Lifeline

BIOGRAPHIES

THE BEATLES

Music Revolutionaries

by Jeremy Roberts

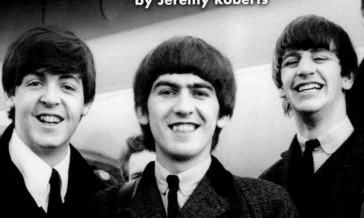

Twenty-First Century Books · Minneapolis

For Bobby—yeah, yeah, yeah . . .

Twenty-First Century Books
A division of Lerner Publishing Group, Inc.
241 First Avenue North
Minneapolis, MN 55401 U.S.A.

Website address: www.lernerbooks.com

Library of Congress Cataloging-in-Publication Data

Roberts, Jeremy, 1956–
    The Beatles : music revolutionaries / by Jeremy Roberts.
        p.   cm. — (USA TODAY lifeline biographies)
    Includes bibliographical references and index.
    ISBN 978-0-7613-6421-4 (lib. bdg. : alk. paper)
    1. Beatles. 2. Rock musicians—England—Biography. I. Title.
ML421.B4R62 2011
782.42166092'2—dc22 [B]   2010031041

Manufactured in the United States of America
1 – VI – 12/31/10

USA TODAY **Lifeline** BIOGRAPHIES

THE BEATLES

Left-handed imitator: Paul McCartney (*above*) already had musical talent when he met John Lennon in 1957. He showed off his skills by imitating Eddie Cochran's playing of "Twenty Flight Rock."

First Encounters

■■■■

The two boys eyed each other. John had just finished playing with his band at a church festival in Liverpool, England. With his hair slicked back and pants pegged tight, he looked like a tough—a "teddy boy" as the look was called. Not yet seventeen, he was the guitarist and leader of a band called the Quarrymen.

Paul briefly glanced at John. He'd dressed up for the festival, trying to impress some girls. Now he found himself trying to impress the band members instead. Someone handed him a guitar. He fingered the strings and cranked into "Twenty Flight Rock," an early hit by American rock 'n' roller Eddie Cochran.

John was impressed, though he barely nodded. Paul followed up with another pop song, then a medley of hits by Little Richard, another American rock musician. Somewhere along the way, Paul played "Long Tall Sally," a Little Richard song he was always working on.

Be-Bop: One of the songs John Lennon *(above)* performed at the Liverpool festival was "Be-Bop-a-Lula" by Gene Vincent. John saw Vincent sing the song in the movie *The Girl Can't Help It*, which also featured Eddie Cochran singing "Twenty Flight Rock."

And that was that. The Quarrymen played another set. Paul turned his attention back to what he'd come to do—pick up girls. He drifted toward the edge of the crowd as the group played, then moved on to the local pub. But this chance meeting in 1957 would change the history of pop music. For the two young men who'd met in the steaming-hot church hall were John Lennon and Paul McCartney. Together, they would become one of music's greatest creative teams. Along with George Harrison and Ringo Starr, they would form The Beatles, one of the most important rock groups ever.

Their songs would be played across the world. People would scream and faint when they performed. While it would take several difficult years of hard work and disappointment, once The Beatles made it, they really made it. They helped define the music we call rock 'n' roll. They also helped define the 1960s.

The sixties were a time of youthful change and creativity—a time of "Revolution," to borrow one of The Beatles' song titles. The Beatles were a major part of that revolution.

The Beatles performed in an era of rapid changes in technology as well as music. Their images were sent by television and radio across the world. For a while, many considered them as famous as God. But the reality of The Beatles was always much larger than the

Screaming fans: Teenage girls laughed, cried, and were in shock at Beatles' concerts.

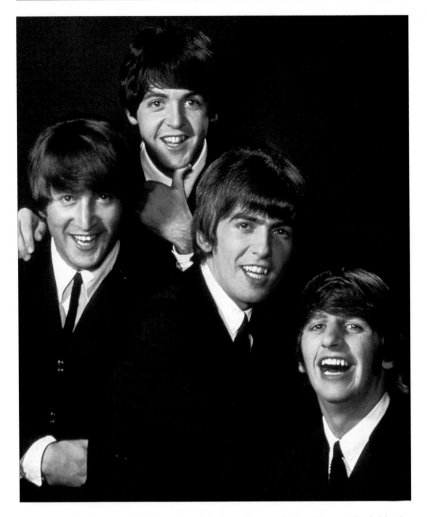

Fab Four: The four musicians enjoyed their early popularity. The media dubbed them the Fab Four. They influenced not only music but fashion, style, and culture as well. From left to right are John Lennon, Paul McCartney, George Harrison, and Ringo Starr.

image generated by and for the media. Their talents were such that nothing could contain them, not even hysteria and hype so crazy it was called Beatlemania. Ironically, that talent—and maybe the sixties themselves—doomed the group in the end.

On the Mersey: All The Beatles hailed from Liverpool. This port city sits on the Mersey River in northwestern England and was hard hit by economic troubles after World War II (1939–1945).

Early Days

Except for their guitars, John Lennon and Paul McCartney didn't seem to have much in common when they met that hot summer day in Liverpool. For one thing, John was almost two years older than Paul. John was born on October 9, 1940. Paul was born on June 18, 1942. John's family was middle class. Paul's was working class. In Britain, at the time, these differences could mean a lot. Some people would not associate with members of a different class.

Young boys: John and Paul *(left and right)* as young boys. They wouldn't meet until they were in their teens, but they had music and the loss of their mothers in common.

There were other differences as well. In school, Paul was a more attentive student. John didn't care about studying, and would cut class, fail his subjects, get into fights, and even steal candy and cigarettes from local merchants, earning him the label of a troublemaker.

On the other hand, the boys had some important things in common. Both had gone through difficult family trials. Paul's mother died from cancer a few months before the pair met. Up until the age of seventeen, John lost nearly every important adult in his life. His father abandoned the family when John was a baby. His mother, Julia, gave John to her sister Mimi and her husband, George Smith, to raise. John loved his uncle George, who died when John was only thirteen. In grief, John turned to his mother, Julia, who lived nearby in a poorer neighborhood. Julia was less strict than his aunt Mimi. His mother played the banjo and bought John his first guitar. A few years later, Julia was waiting for a bus when a speeding driver hit and killed her.

Aunt Mimi: During much of his childhood, John lived with his aunt, Mimi Smith *(right).* She was strict and straightforward, and she loved her nephew dearly.

Both boys grew up in families and a city that had seen better days. Located at the mouth of the Mersey River in northwestern England, Liverpool had many factories as well as an important seaport. The Germans had bombed much of the city during World War II. It was rebuilt after the war, but changes in the economy in Britain and the world made Liverpool less important than it had once been. By the 1950s, many of its industries were struggling or had moved away. The city's many working-class people often had a hard time finding jobs and paying for necessities.

Still, Liverpool was an important port for ships traveling to and from the United States. Americans often came to the city, bringing with them American goods, American music, and American ideas. Because it was an industrial city as well as a seaport, Liverpool had a reputation as a tough place, much as American cities such as Pittsburgh and Detroit do.

Both the American influence and the tough-guy image would be important to Lennon and McCartney as they honed their musical skills.

The fact that Liverpool was relatively far from London also played a role in Lennon and McCartney's future. At the time, the important British recording companies were located in London. Many people there looked down on musical groups from outside the city, especially those from working-class towns such as Liverpool. This attitude presented one more barrier for the young musicians to overcome.

IN FCUS

Working-Class Life

Throughout its history, British society had been divided into strict social classes: upper class (kings and noble families); middle class (educated people, skilled craftspeople, business owners); and peasants or lower classes (farmers, servants and, later, factory workers). People born to the lower classes had a hard time moving up in the world.

When The Beatles were growing up, the lower classes were split into working class and the poor. Paul McCartney's father sold cotton cloth. George Harrison's dad drove a bus. Ringo's father worked in a bakery, and his stepfather painted houses. Their families lived in government-run council houses, built to replace buildings that had been bombed into rubble during World War II. Ringo grew up in the Dingle, one of Liverpool's poorest neighborhoods. John Lennon's real father was a working-class waiter, but John lived in a middle-class neighborhood with his aunt Mimi and uncle George, who owned a dairy business. Aunt Mimi tried to stop John from playing with working-class boys, but John preferred their company.

Many working-class families dreamed of seeing their children move into the middle class. The Beatles and their families were able to achieve that and more because of the group's success.

The most important things John Lennon and Paul McCartney had in common were their creativity and intelligence. Once they met, they egged each other on to improve their musical skills and learn more. Something sparked in that hot church hall in 1957. It quickly grew into a raging inferno. "That was the day," Lennon later said, "the day I met Paul, that it started moving." A few days later, Lennon had a friend ask McCartney if he'd care to join the Quarrymen.

Skiffle

The Quarrymen were named after Quarry Bank Grammar School, the school the original members attended. The band played skiffle, a cross between American bluegrass, country, rhythm and blues, and early rock 'n' roll music. A British style, skiffle had a primitive sound that featured musicians playing banjos and household items such as washboards.

Washboards were used to clean clothes in the days before families had home washing machines. Rubbing a hard object across the surface of a washboard produced a shuffling-kind of percussion sound.

The teenage Quarrymen weren't very good at first. John Lennon didn't even know how to tune his guitar when Paul met him. But they were willing to learn, and they put in long hours practicing and listening to rock 'n' roll music. Learning was an adventure. One day, McCartney and Lennon journeyed by bus across the city to meet a guitarist who could show them how to play B7, a common guitar chord in rock music. Another day, they hunted down someone with a hard-to-find American record.

Most people, including their relatives, didn't think much of music as a career. Paul's father had played piano and trumpet with his own band during the 1920s. But he gave up music for a steady job in the cotton trade, where he worked as a salesman after the war. John's aunt, Mimi Smith, was a strict and loving guardian. She allowed him to practice guitar and start a band, but she wasn't enthusiastic about music. "A guitar's all right," she used to tell him. "But you'll never earn your living by it."

George, Stu, and the Silver Beatles

As John and Paul got better, so did the Quarrymen. At some point in 1958, Paul convinced John to let another friend, George Harrison, join the group. Born on February 25, 1943, Harrison was the youngest member of the band, but he was already good enough on the guitar to play lead. His father was a bus driver and union official.

His mother, interested in music and dance, did everything she could to encourage her son's interest in the guitar.

The other original members of the Quarrymen soon found other interests and left the band. But John, Paul, and George continued to play together and hone their craft. They also continued to go to school. Paul and George went to high school at the Liverpool Institute. John attended the Liverpool Art College, located next door to the high school.

Lead guitarist: George Harrison *(above)* already was showing musical promise when he was a boy. Unlike John and Paul, who were mostly self-taught, George had taken guitar lessons.

Getting together: By 1960 George *(left)*, John *(middle)*, and Paul *(right)* were regularly playing and hanging out together.

The trio all played guitars. They added a bass guitar player when John convinced a friend named Stuart Sutcliffe to join them. Stu was a talented painter—he had even sold one of his paintings for a large sum of money. He couldn't play the bass very well, but he was a friend of John's and helped fill out the band's sound as it continued to grow.

Somewhere along the way, the teenagers started calling themselves the Silver Beatles. The origin of the name seems hazy, even to the band members. Recalling their early days, John, Paul, and George usually told writers that the inspiration had come from an American rock group, Buddy Holly and the Crickets. Changing the spelling of the insect name "beetles" to "Beatles" made for a pun on the word *beat*, as early rock 'n' roll was sometimes called.

But Paul told biographer Barry Miles that the name might actually have come from a movie. "We were into the Marlon Brando film *The Wild One*," he recalled. "And in that they use the word *beetles*, and we think that kind of clinched it."

The band thought the beetles were members of Brando's motorcycle gang. But the nickname actually referred to the bikers' girlfriends.

The Silver Beatles played a variety of dance halls and rough clubs in the Liverpool area for little pay. They toured Scotland. They even played during a striptease act. As they struggled, they got better, learning by doing—and doing and doing and doing.

Most of the tunes that the Silver Beatles played were called covers—songs by other artists. The problem was that sometimes other bands who played first would play the same songs the Silver Beatles planned to do. "Once they'd done four or five of them," Paul recalled later, "we'd go: 'There goes our set list!' I remember saying, 'We've got to write our own [songs], because then they won't be able to access them.' " That's when Lennon and McCartney began to collaborate on songwriting.

The important musical influences on the group were all American: Elvis Presley, Buddy Holly, Little Richard, Jerry Lee Lewis, and Chuck Berry, to name a few. Their music had a harder edge and beat than the most popular groups of the time. In Britain, for example, Cliff Richard and the Shadows emphasized a softer, more melodic approach to rock and pop ballads.

Best on Drums

Still raw, the band slowly gathered fans. They had one serious problem, however. They lacked a steady drummer. Different drummers played with them on occasion, but for many of their gigs in 1959 and 1960, they played without any drums at all. In the summer of 1960, Paul called up Pete Best, a drummer who had played with them at times in the past. Pete's mother owned a small Liverpool club called the Casbah, where the band had played on and off since it opened in the summer of 1959.

"Paul said had I still got any drums," Best remembered later. "I told him I'd just got a complete new kit.... He said they'd got a job in Hamburg [Germany] and was I interested in being their drummer? ... I'd get [fifteen pounds] a week, which was a lot [of money]. Much better than going to a training college."

At the time, fifteen pounds a week was considered a decent workingman's pay. For a teenager who wanted to be a musician, it was a fortune.

"Make Show"

If Liverpool had a reputation for being a tough town, Hamburg's reputation was ten times worse. And the German city lived up—or down—to that reputation. Gunrunning smugglers, gangsters, and prostitutes—you could find them all in the area of clubs and bars known as the St. Pauli district. Exactly the place for a green and growing rock 'n' roll band to learn its trade. To the Silver Beatles, Hamburg looked like the big time.

During the fall of 1960, the Silver Beatles performed long, grinding sets in the St. Pauli district. They started in a bar called the Indra, known for its violent brawls. According to rock historians Bob Cepican and Waleed Ali, at least one shooting occurred at the Indra while the Silver Beatles performed there. The police soon closed the Indra, and the band moved on to the Kaiserkeller, another bar owned by the same man.

The German audience liked the group's rough sound and their tough-guy act. John would insult the crowd and do crazy things like giving the outlawed Nazi salute. They would joke between sets and interact with the audience. Bruno Koschmider, the club owner, encouraged them to *mach schau*—"make show." Their wild performances were good for business.

Somewhere along the way, the group dropped "Silver" from its name. The German audiences loved to pronounce *Beatles* as *peedles*, which punned into a dirty word. The Beatles didn't mind. "We used to do crazy things because we were identified as the *Verrückt* Beatles, which was the crazy Beatles," Pete Best said later. "John would split his jeans and there would be mock fights onstage. We'd jump off the stage and dance with the audience and run around and stamp our feet. . . . The faster the music, the faster the German crowd went wild."

But a lot more was going on. The Beatles honed their act. Their music got tighter. They learned how to please people with a combination of

By Astrid : The Beatles' German friend Astrid Kirchherr took this picture of the band at a Hamburg amusement park in 1960. The photo includes drummer Pete Best *(far left)* and bass guitarist Stu Sutcliffe *(far right)*. Note that the boys hadn't yet adopted their signature hairstyle.

humor and attitude that complemented the music. "They suddenly found that there was something different from playing for the rest of their lives in Liverpool," said Billy Harry, who covered the Liverpool music scene in his newspaper, the *Mersey Beat*. "I don't think they thought of big success before that time. . . . They were so excited. They weren't swollen heads; it was enthusiasm."

Among the people they met were three young Germans—Jurgen Vollmer, Astrid Kirchherr, and Klaus Voormann. The three had gone to school together and shared an interest in photography, music, culture, and fashion. While exploring the St. Pauli district, Voormann heard The Beatles' unusual sound and encouraged Vollmer and Kirchherr to listen to the music. All three became very interested in the group and went to hear them frequently. Kirchherr and Vollmer eventually took a number of photographs of the group in their leather gear, with their slicked-back hair.

October 1, 1997

How photographer clicked
with the early Beatles

From the Pages of
USA TODAY

Jurgen Vollmer was just the teen-age fan of a teen-age band. He became a sought-after movie and celebrity photographer; they became The Beatles.

Now Vollmer, who befriended The Beatles in Hamburg in 1960, has finally gathered his stylish photographs of the early, pre-Ringo Beatles in an expensive new book, titled *Jurgen Vollmer: From Hamburg to Hollywood.*

"I was a teen-ager and I am also a very shy person, and George Harrison was a little shy and a teen-ager," recalls Vollmer. "He was a nice and sweet person. John Lennon had a little arrogant sneer, and he made all these ironic comments; he didn't put you at ease. But it was an act. Once I got to know him better, he was a softy. He projected that rough and tough rocker image. He wasn't at all, but he fooled me in the beginning. Paul McCartney actually was always nice. He was smiling. He was a gentleman par excellence." Vollmer captured it all in his black-and-white shots.

—Andy Seiler

By Jurgen: Another German friend Jurgen Vollmer shot a photo of John, Paul, and George playing live in Hamburg in 1961.

The Beatles' time in Hamburg came to a crashing conclusion in December 1960, when George was deported from Germany because he was underage. Shortly afterward, Paul McCartney and Pete Best were arrested. Police charged that they had started a small fire in the basement of a theater. Details of what happened vary, but Paul and Pete were told to leave the country. John quickly followed. Stu had become engaged to Kirchherr and decided to stay in Germany.

Rockin' Liverpool

The band had left Liverpool as teenagers trying to figure out how to play music. They came back to Britain confirmed rock 'n' rollers. Dressed in leather, interspersing humor with their sharp rock 'n' roll, The Beatles had a unique image and sound. The uniqueness quickly became apparent at the Cavern Club, a large, sweltering basement

At the Cavern: After their return to Liverpool from Hamburg in 1960, the band became a regular draw at the Cavern Club. Young people and workers gathered there to hear local bands.

club in downtown Liverpool. They won a standing lunchtime gig there. Within a few weeks, they had a dedicated following.

Their song lineup included a number of original compositions written by John and Paul. These tunes caught the energy and vitality of their roaring stage show. The lyrics had a bouncy playfulness that became their trademark. Creatively, the songs were miles ahead of the music the band had performed just a few months before.

The Beatles returned to Hamburg in April 1961 and stayed for thirteen weeks, playing to wildly enthusiastic audiences. While Stuart sat in on some of the performances, at least at the beginning, Paul took over as bass player. He wasn't enthusiastic about it at first. Little did he know that he would become the most famous bass player in rock history.

"I definitely didn't want to do it, but Stuart left," said Paul, "and I got lumbered with it." John couldn't play bass, and George played lead guitar, so it was up to Paul to learn.

"Paul was one of the most innovative bass players that ever played bass," said John many years later. "Not technically great," Lennon added. "None of us were technical musicians. None of us could read music. None of us can write it. But as pure musicians, as inspired humans to make noise [we're] as good as anyone!"

Playing monster sets from seven at night to two in the morning, The Beatles continued to polish their act in Germany. They appeared for a while with Tony Sheridan, a well-known British guitarist and singer. With Sheridan, they recorded a few songs, including a rock version of "My Bonnie Lies Over the Ocean," a popular song written in 1881.

Generally, the group lined up with George on lead guitar, John on rhythm guitar, and Paul on bass. John and Paul alternated lead vocals. Their music combined the "hard" style of performers like Chuck Berry with pleasing melodies and prominent harmonies—the blending of different voices. While they wrote some of their own songs, The Beatles played a wide range of covers. Their versatility would be a trademark for the rest of their careers.

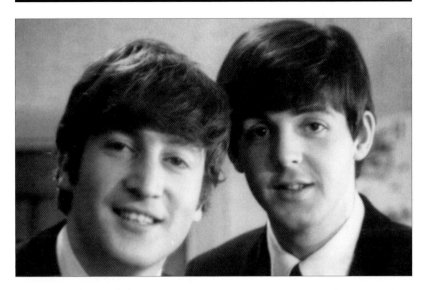

Mop tops: John and Paul show off their mop tops—a hairstyle that many other bands of the 1960s would later imitate.

Back in Liverpool at the beginning of July, The Beatles once again played the Cavern and similar clubs. That fall, John and Paul took a brief vacation to Paris, France. When they returned, they were wearing their hair brushed forward with a straight trim, a cut sometimes called the French style. It would soon become known as The Beatles' style.

 Jurgen Vollmer and Astrid Kirchherr were both given credit for The Beatles hairstyle, but it was actually already popular in their circle of friends. Stu was the first to ask Kirchherr to cut his hair to match the German style, worn by Vollmer and Astrid's boyfriend Klaus Voorman. Later, she cut George's hair. Vollmer says he gave John and Paul the same haircut while they were in Paris.

Pete's in: In 1961, when The Beatles met businessman Brian Epstein for the first time, Pete Best *(second from left)* was still the band's drummer.

"Please Please Me"

Neatly dressed in a well-tailored suit, Brian Epstein descended the steep steps to a dank, dark cellar full of noise. The businessman clutched his briefcase handle firmly. He was shy by nature, and this was not the kind of place he went to often. The Liverpool bar was filled with rowdy rock 'n' roll fans. Most of them were much younger than he was. Many were decidedly not the kind of people his well-to-do family associated with.

But Epstein had a mission this late fall day in 1961. He was going to sell himself to the four leather-clad musicians on the Cavern stage. Brian Epstein, who ran the record division of his family's department store, had only just recently heard of The Beatles when three different customers asked to buy their recording of "My Bonnie Lies Over the Ocean." Epstein did not have the record, but when

Someone new: Epstein was well spoken and well educated and had once thought about being an actor. His self-confidence and sales skills were just what the band needed.

someone told him the band was playing in the neighborhood, he decided to check them out. Impressed with their sound, he decided to ask The Beatles if he could be their manager.

Epstein had to fight his way to the stage. Finally, he reached George Harrison. He shook hands and said he wanted to discuss something after the show. Maybe he could help the group, he added, not explaining how. Harrison took the message to the others. Later in the day, they showed up in the department store. "Quite simply, you need a manager," Epstein told them after he led them past the displays of appliances. "Would you like me to do it?" They said yes.

"Eppy"

Born September 19, 1934, Brian Epstein was the oldest son of a well-known Jewish family in Liverpool. While he had studied for a while to be an actor, Epstein clearly had a talent for business management. He took over the record division of his family's store in late 1957. He did so well that record sales became the most profitable part of the business. He soon opened a second store in the neighborhood near the Cavern. Although Brian was a serious fan of classical music, he stocked a lot of popular music and started writing a column on rock 'n' roll for the *Mersey Beat*.

The *Mersey Beat* was a music-focused newspaper out of Liverpool. Bill Harry, who had gone to art school with John, founded the paper in the early 1960s. Coverage included stories about many Liverpool bands, but the paper also got exclusive interviews and photos of The Beatles that no other publication did.

The majority of Liverpool's residents were Christians, so his religion made Brian different. But he was also different because he was homosexual, or gay. In the 1960s, gay people faced heavy discrimination. The Beatles knew Epstein was gay, and they respected him and valued him tremendously as a manager, and in some ways as a father figure.

Epstein had never managed a musical group before. His inexperience would lead him to make mistakes. On the other hand, he was intelligent and creative. He was able to oversee and coordinate many details to get a job done. He had a knack for figuring out what people wanted, and he was a good salesman. He also had complete and total faith in The Beatles.

Epstein had two short-range goals. The first was to increase the amount of money The Beatles received for shows. This he did by finding new places for them to play. His second goal was to get them a record contract with a major company. Without records, The Beatles' music would never reach a large audience. Nor would they make much money.

Because Epstein ran a successful record store, he knew many people in the music industry. But most of these people were in sales. The people who made records worked in different divisions. They were difficult to reach, let alone persuade. Still, Epstein was able to use his contacts to get a few record company scouts to listen to The Beatles. Most didn't think The Beatles had what it took to succeed. They recorded demos (recordings made to help sell the band to record producers) in January 1962. Epstein met with representatives of Decca, a large record company that distributed Elvis Presley's records in Britain. "Not to mince words, Mr. Epstein, we don't like your boys' sound," said one of the officials. "Groups are out; four-piece groups with guitars particularly are finished."

"You must be out of your mind," Epstein responded. "You get these boys on TV and you will have an explosion. I am completely confident that one day they will be bigger than Elvis Presley."

Epstein knew that the hard-core rebel look wasn't popular with audiences outside Liverpool—or with the record companies. So he convinced The Beatles to wear specially tailored mohair suits with narrow

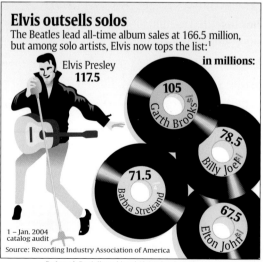

USA TODAY Snapshots®

Elvis outsells solos

The Beatles lead all-time album sales at 166.5 million, but among solo artists, Elvis now tops the list:[1]

in millions:

Elvis Presley
117.5

105
Garth Brooks

78.5
Billy Joel

71.5
Barbra Streisand

67.5
Elton John

1 – Jan. 2004 catalog audit

Source: Recording Industry Association of America

By Joseph Popiolkowski and Alejandro Gonzalez, USA TODAY, 2004

LPs, 33s, 45s

Before CDs and digital downloads were invented, people listened to records. Hard vinyl disks were stamped with a long, spiraling groove and played on a revolving turntable. A thin arm fitted with a needle rested on the rotating vinyl disk to produce sound waves, which were further amplified by a set of speakers. Long-playing records of five to eight songs, called LPs, or albums, rotated at 33 revolutions per minute. Short records with one song per side, called singles, or 45s, rotated at 45 revolutions per minute.

lapels. Although the suits clashed with The Beatles' rough image and rebellious personalities, the band members agreed to wear them. They also tightened their stage act.

Perseverance

Neither the cleaner look nor better demos convinced anyone to sign the group. But Epstein kept at it. Finally that May, he contacted George Martin, a producer at a record label called Parlophone. Though Parlophone's parent company, EMI, had turned down The Beatles, Martin hadn't been involved in that decision. He agreed to have The Beatles audition for him.

At this time, The Beatles were in Hamburg for a series of shows there. When they arrived, they learned that their friend and former bandmate, Stu Sutcliffe, had died. He'd had a brain hemorrhage, perhaps as a result of injuries from a fight after a show more than a year earlier. The band members were shocked and saddened, but the news of the audition lifted their spirits. John and Paul wrote a song called "Love Me Do" to play at the audition.

Martin didn't seem impressed when they played. He would "let them know," he said. The Beatles had heard that before. More than a month later, however, Martin told Brian Epstein that he'd like to take a chance on the group. New groups usually put out a single or two first. If people liked the singles, the group would then make a full album. Martin offered to record and release a single for The Beatles.

Martin didn't offer to pay much. The Beatles would earn an English farthing, or one-quarter penny, for each record they sold. Still, the opportunity was great news to Epstein and The Beatles. Martin had one condition, however. They'd have to have a different drummer record with them in the studio. Pete Best wasn't good enough.

"Pete Forever, Ringo Never"

John, Paul, and George had had doubts about Pete Best for some time. When Brian Epstein told them that George Martin wanted to bring in a new drummer, the band members came to their own decision—Pete was out. In his place, they wanted a drummer named Richard Starkey, known as Ringo Starr. And they wanted Brian to break the news to Pete.

Brian did, the morning after a show—and before Pete knew that

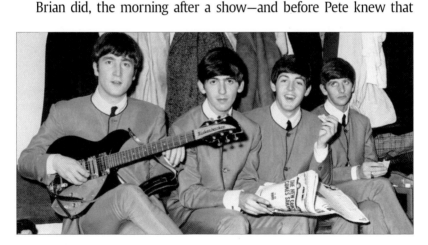

Ringo's in: Experienced rock drummer Ringo Starr *(far right)* joined The Beatles in 1962. He'd known the band members for several years, having played in Hamburg's clubs alongside other Liverpool bands, including The Beatles.

IN FOCUS

George Martin

Often called the "Fifth Beatle," producer George Martin was an important part of The Beatles' success. Born on January 3, 1926, he started taking piano lessons when he was eight. As a young man, he dreamed of becoming a great pianist and composer. During World War II, he joined the Royal Navy and became a pilot. Following the war, he completed school and went to work for the BBC, Britain's broadcasting company, then EMI, a major record company. At first, he worked on classical music, recording it and turning it into albums. Gradually, he began working on other types of recordings, including comedy.

By the time he met The Beatles, Martin was the head of Parlophone Records, a small label owned by EMI. Besides overseeing the recording and mixing of The Beatles' songs, Martin occasionally added piano parts and helped transcribe song parts for performers. For example, he plays the piano on the song "Lovely Rita."

Fifth Beatle: George Martin was in his mid-thirties when he began producing The Beatles records.

The Beatles were a big part but not the only part of Martin's career. He produced many albums in many genres. He also composed his own music, including part of the sound track of *Live and Let Die* (1973), a famous James Bond movie. In recognition of his contributions to music and Britain, Martin was knighted by the queen in 1996, making him Sir George Martin.

the group had been offered a recording contract. He was shocked. So were the fans. Girls camped out in front of Best's home. Banners all over Liverpool proclaimed "Pete Forever, Ringo Never," but they did no good.

Hair fix: To join the band, Ringo had to reshape his hairstyle to match the others' mop tops. The effort covered up a premature gray patch on his right temple.

Ringo Starr began drumming in 1956, at the age of sixteen, as part of a band called the Eddie Clayton Skiffle Group. Around 1959 he joined Rory Storm and the Raving Texans, later known as the Hurricanes. Until 1961 they were better known—and better paid—than The Beatles.

Ringo had a good sense of humor, had experience playing to big crowds, and was a decent rock drummer. He also had a great deal of stamina, important for live performances. He could carry the beat through a long, grinding gig.

Rory Storm & the Hurricanes had played in Hamburg in 1961. Ringo even played with The Beatles occasionally. So it was natural for them to turn to him when they kicked out Pete Best in August 1962. Ringo didn't know that the group was about to make music history. His decision to join them was purely practical. "I got another offer at the same time, from Kingsize Taylor & the Dominoes," Ringo said some years

According to Philip Norman (who wrote the book *Shout!*), Ringo's bandmates in the Hurricanes called him Rings and then Ringo because he wore so many rings. Starkey was changed to Starr, adds Norman, so that the Hurricanes could bill his drum solo as "Starr Time."

later. "He offered twenty pounds a week. The Beatles offered twenty-five, so I took them."

A Hit

The Beatles' years of hard work were starting to pay off in a big way. At the same time, John Lennon's relationship with his girlfriend, Cynthia Powell, took its own turn. Cynthia told him she was pregnant. "Don't worry, Cyn," he told her when he found out. "We'll get married."

Lennon's aunt Mimi had a screaming fit when he told her about the situation. But she eventually gave him the money for a gold wedding ring. With help from Brian Epstein and with Paul McCartney as a witness, the pair were married on August 23, 1962.

Their son, Julian, named after John's mother, was born on April 8, 1963. While John's marriage wasn't a secret, it wasn't publicized either. Epstein knew that an important part of The Beatles' image, specifically for female fans, was sex appeal. Married men didn't sell.

The first Beatles' single, "Love Me Do," was released soon after the marriage, on October 5, 1962. "The first time I heard 'Love Me Do' on the radio, I went shivery all over," recalled George Harrison. He'd stayed up all night to hear the record broadcast on Radio Luxembourg, a popular outlet for new pop songs at the time.

The record received decent airtime on the radio and did well on the charts, the rankings of pop record sales. It moved slowly to the number seventeen spot—good for a new group. "I didn't think [the song] was all that brilliant, but I was very thrilled by the reaction to The Beatles and their sound," recalled George Martin. "The problem now was to get a follow-up record for them."

Martin suggested a song written by someone else, but The Beatles didn't like it. They wanted to record their own songs. This idea was somewhat unusual at the time. Most groups used music from different writers, always searching for a hit. Martin challenged the band to come up with a song as good as the one he had suggested. So Lennon and McCartney went to work.

IN FOCUS

Writing the Songs

John Lennon and Paul McCartney wrote most of The Beatles' songs, including nearly every song that is considered a classic. From the very beginning to the very end of the band's existence, their songs were authored as "Lennon-McCartney."

While the credit was always the same, not every song was written the same way. Some were true collaborations, which Paul and John worked out together. Others were composed mostly by just Paul or by just John, with the other one helping to fill out the music or words later on. Although the two songwriters often had different approaches, they were somehow able to make their songs harmonious.

John's songs had a harder edge. His attitude could be bitter or even angry. His lyrics often came from his personal experiences. Paul's music tended to be more melodic and pleasing to the ear. His songs generally had a musical hook—a catchy sound or chorus. Both songwriters learned from each other and criticized and helped improve each other's work. "My contribution to Paul's songs was always to add a little bluesy edge to them . . . . He provided a lightness, an optimism, while I would always go for the sadness, the discords, the bluesy notes," said John.

"One of the best things about Lennon and McCartney," Paul told an interviewer, "was the competitive element within the team. It was great. I could do stuff he might not be in the mood for, egg him in a certain direction he might not want to go in. And he could do the same for me."

"Had John never met Paul, and vice versa, I firmly believe that neither of them would have turned out to be the great songwriters that they were," added producer George Martin. "They would have been good, but not blisteringly great, as millions of us think they are. Each had a tremendous influence on the other, which neither of them consciously realized."

On November 26, 1962, they came back from an engagement in Hamburg to record "Please Please Me." The record was released in January 1963. Within a few weeks, it was the country's number one pop song. The Beatles had become the hottest band in Great Britain.

Noise control: Police officers routinely helped to control British Beatles' fans, like these in Manchester, England, in 1963.

Beatlemania

Describing a tornado is easy—if you're a few miles away. If you're in the middle of the storm, though, it's hard to say exactly what's going on. You pitch and whirl, carried around by the wind. You have no control. The best you can do is go along for the ride.

The Beatles were caught up in a tornado in 1963. They didn't know it at first. When they realized what was happening, all they could do was hold on for the ride. Their talent and hard work helped make it all possible. But other forces were also at work. No one could have predicted the wild craziness that seemed to consume all of Britain in 1963. Suddenly, everyone had to have a Beatles' album. Suddenly, everyone had to hear them. And see them. And touch them.

A Beatles' Storm

The single "Please Please Me" marched to the top of the sales charts in February 1963. On February 11, the group hunkered down in EMI's London studios to record a full album. From roughly ten in the morning to eleven at night, with only a few short breaks, they laid down the tracks for a fourteen-song LP. "What I tried to do was to create the live pop group on tape," said Norman Smith, the recording engineer. "I tried to get the sound of The Beatles singing and playing as they'd perform onstage. I thought if I didn't do it, I'd lose the excitement."

The last song in the session—and the last song on the album—was "Twist and Shout," popularized by the Isley Brothers, an African American group regarded as rhythm and blues pioneers. The Beatles had often used the song to end their shows at the Cavern. "John absolutely screamed it," said George Martin. "God knows what it did to his larynx because it made a

First records: The band works with George Martin *(seated)* during an early recording session.

sound like tearing flesh." Lennon's screams were combined with the rising vocal harmonies and the song's driving beat. While the band may have been tired by the time the session was over, the raw energy of their live shows still came through.

Released on March 22, 1963, the album, also called *Please Please Me*, shot to number one on the British charts and

Please Please Me: The song "Please Please Me" became the cornerstone of The Beatles' first album *(above)*. John was intrigued by using the word *please* in the title in two different meanings.

stayed there for thirty weeks. Besides the title song, other works included "I Saw Her Standing There," "Love Me Do," and "Do You Want to Know a Secret." All were destined to become Beatles' anthems.

Before and after the album came out, The Beatles played a grueling schedule of live performances. Sometimes they played two concerts in the same day. They performed on a series of radio shows. They made many television appearances. They often raced from an interview to a show, traveling more than 100 miles (161 kilometers) in a few hours.

In July they began recording a new album, *With The Beatles*, which

Through the media, the four Beatles got individual nicknames. John was The Smart One. George, who rarely spoke up in interviews, was dubbed The Quiet One. Paul was The Cute One. And Ringo, whose wry sense of humor interviewers had come to expect, was The Funny One.

was released in November. Before it came out, record stores ordered three hundred thousand copies—a huge advance order in Britain. But even that amount wasn't enough as the record soared up the charts.

The media only added to the band's popularity. Live performances on radio brought their music to mass audiences. In the newspapers, story after story kept them in front of the public. Writers gave them clever nicknames, such as the Fab Four. Another nickname, lovable mop tops, referred to the band members' haircuts. At a time when most men and boys wore crew cuts or other close-cropped styles, The Beatles' hair was considered quite long and even a little outrageous. The style quickly caught on among their teenage fans.

In October the group appeared on *Sunday Night at the London Palladium*, the most popular television show in Britain at the time. The Beatles played five songs and made themselves well known to the public. Before the show, a large group of teenagers gathered outside,

Playing the Palladium: In October 1963, The Beatles were the lead act on a popular TV show, *Sunday Night at the London Palladium*. "Playing the Palladium"—a historic theater in London's West End—was the goal of many musical performers.

Along the way, the band picked up two road managers—Neil Aspinall and Mal Evans. Neil had gone to school with Paul and George. He owned the van that The Beatles used to get to gigs. Mal had been a bouncer at the Cavern and was an early fan.

hoping to see the band. About fifty of them managed to break into the auditorium and surround The Beatles during their rehearsal. The media played up the event the next day. One newspaper, the *London Daily Mirror*, called the fans' chaos "Beatlemania." The word would soon be used over and over again.

Any doubts about their popularity were banished when they were invited to perform for the Queen Mother (the mother of the reigning Queen Elizabeth II) and other members of the royal family in early November. Known as the *Royal Variety Performance*, the televised show was very important in Britain. Getting invited was an honor and an opportunity. In the space of four songs, The Beatles won the British royalty as fans. Their appearance also showed how important teenage music—and teens in general—had suddenly become. The invitation to play for the Queen Mother meant that The Beatles' music was being taken seriously, not dismissed as something just for kids. The Beatles and their fans had come of age.

Before beginning the last son, John joked with the audience, asking those "in the cheaper seats, clap your hands. And the rest of you, if you'd just rattle your jewelry." Lennon's joke got a laugh at the show and was repeated in the newspapers the next day. The remark was a comment on the different classes in Britain. The rich and aristocratic—including the queen—lived separately from the working class, or commoners. Lennon's joke was called "cheeky"—brash and a little irreverent. But this attitude was part of The Beatles' attraction for young

For the Queen Mum: Elizabeth, the Queen Mother, greets the band members after they performed for her in the *Royal Variety Performance* in November 1963.

people. The band members seemed like rebels, and many young people were filled with rebellious spirit.

On the other hand, The Beatles could be irreverent without threatening people. They seemed friendly and happy. They were always joking and making fun, especially of themselves. The suits that Brian Epstein insisted they wear helped make them acceptable, as well as instantly recognizable. And their songs were appealing. After all, they were all about love.

The Beatles' hit songs reversed "the tiresome trend towards weepie lost-love wailers," an EMI press release explained. The songs were "happy-go-lucky," continued the press release. A writer for the *Daily Mirror* summed up the group's appeal this way: "You have to be a real sour square not to love the nutty, noisy, happy handsome Beatles."

Across the Ocean

By late 1963, The Beatles were the top rock act in Great Britain. They had two number one albums and drew large crowds wherever they played. Their fame went beyond the music world. Nearly everyone seemed to know who they were, thanks to hundreds and hundreds of news stories about them. Their music was innovative and influential, a British twist on American rock 'n' roll. Music writers even compared John and Paul to Beethoven, ranking them among the greatest composers of all time.

But they were barely known in the United States. It wasn't because they hadn't tried. Four Beatles' singles had been released in the United States, but none had sold very well. Many people felt that the "English sound" didn't appeal to American ears. Brian Epstein was determined to make The Beatles as big in the United States as they were in Britain. Because the United States was so much larger than Britain, any band that succeeded in the United States could make a lot of money. And because rock 'n' roll had started in the United States, winning over American fans was the true test for any rock musician.

In November 1963, Brian Epstein arranged for a New York City concert. He also managed to get Capitol Records to agree to release Beatles' albums in the United States. Capitol was a large company and had a better chance than the others for good sales. Most important, Epstein struck a deal to get The Beatles on *The Ed Sullivan Show*.

During The Beatles' era, *The Ed Sullivan Show* was one of the most popular television programs in the United States. Millions of families tuned in every Sunday night to see all sorts of acts—circus acrobats, comics, sports legends, lion tamers, ballerinas, scenes from Broadway musicals, classical musicians, rock 'n' roll singers, and even puppeteers. The variety show ran from 1948 to 1971.

The deal Epstein struck with the show was not very good financially. But it guaranteed that The Beatles would be the headline act for two shows, the first in February 1964. That arrangement would give them prestige as well as a big audience.

In early January, to set up their American visit, The Beatles released "I Want to Hold Your Hand" as a single in the United States. The song made the American list of the top one hundred hits but just barely.

The next week, it hit forty-two.

The third week, it went to number one.

Beatlemania was about to sweep the United States.

On Top of the World

As they landed at Kennedy Airport in New York, The Beatles looked out the windows of their Pan Am airliner. The terminal building was swarming with fans. The band was used to this sort of crowd in Britain, but they were surprised to see it in the United States, where they'd never been. They were awed. Inside the terminal, reporters mobbed the group in a mad rush.

Beatle maniacs: In New York, fans of The Beatles waited outside the Plaza Hotel in hopes of seeing the band during their first U.S. tour in 1964.

The Beatles joked with the reporters, in what would become their typical fashion:

Reporter: Will you sing for us?

Beatles: No!

Reporter: Is it because you can't sing?

John: We need money first.

Reporter: Why do you sing like Americans but speak with an English accent?

John: It sells better.

Reporter: Are you in favor of lunacy?

Paul: It's healthy.

Ed Sullivan had his largest audience ever when The Beatles played their first show. Teenagers in the auditorium, especially the girls, screamed all through the act. Those watching at home sat glued to their TV sets. People everywhere talked about the group the next day.

With Ed: Ed Sullivan *(middle)* introduced The Beatles to a nationwide U.S. audience on February 9, 1964, on *The Ed Sullivan Show.* About 73 million viewers tuned in—more than 40 percent of the U.S. population.

American girls tried to decide which Beatle was the cutest. There was a rush on jelly beans, which George had mentioned he liked. Both Ed Sullivan concerts were wildly successful.

"What happened in the States was just like Britain, only ten times bigger," said Ringo. The press coverage, the crowds, and the record sales—everything multiplied. And success in the United States meant The Beatles were now an international phenomenon.

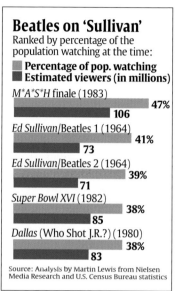

Beatles on 'Sullivan'
Ranked by percentage of the population watching at the time:
■ **Percentage of pop. watching**
■ **Estimated viewers (in millions)**

M*A*S*H finale (1983)
47%
106

Ed Sullivan/Beatles 1 (1964)
41%
73

Ed Sullivan/Beatles 2 (1964)
39%
71

Super Bowl XVI (1982)
38%
85

Dallas (Who Shot J.R.?) (1980)
38%
83

Source: Analysis by Martin Lewis from Nielsen Media Research and U.S. Census Bureau statistics

By Suzy Parker, USA TODAY, 2004

Why?

Other groups and performers, from Frank Sinatra to Elvis Presley, had attracted large, hysterical crowds of teenagers. But The Beatles and Beatlemania seemed to go beyond anything that had happened before. The crowds were larger and stayed longer. The group's impact reached further into society. The craziness was, well, crazier. Why? The answer can't be easily summed up.

Some critics contend that The Beatles came to the United States at a low point for American pop music. There was no one dominant super group at the time. Innovators such as Chuck Berry had done their best work years before. Some rockers, such as Jerry Lee Lewis, had earned bad reputations because of personal scandals. Other rock musicians, such as Buddy Holly, had died young. The Beatles helped fill a musical void, some critics say, even if no one realized there was a void at the time.

Another important factor was the music itself. Many popular performers of the early 1960s—including Roy Orbison, Sam Cooke, and Frankie Valli and the Four Seasons—were known for slow and sad love songs. In contrast, Beatles' songs were filled with energy, a refreshing change from the slower songs. The words were bouncy and fresh. The sound was polished and fun. But The Beatles' appeal went beyond music. For one thing, they were sex symbols. Teenage girls—and in some cases their older sisters and mothers—were especially attracted by their hair, their clothes, their good looks, and their fame. But they were also safe and friendly sex symbols—not hard-edged troublemakers like some early rock 'n' rollers. And their image as fun-loving kids made them popular with everyone, not just women.

While The Beatles appealed to people in all age groups, their main audience was teenagers. And the size of that audience was another reason for Beatlemania. After World War II, many soldiers returned home to the United States, Britain, and other countries and started families. Lots of babies were born in a population swell that came to be called the baby boom. The early baby boomers were teenagers when The Beatles became popular. So one reason the craziness was larger was simply because there were more people to be crazy.

When The Beatles became popular, many baby boomers identified with them. Teenagers saw and heard their own energy and enthusiasm in The Beatles and their music. They saw and heard their own attitudes in The Beatles' performances and songs, and they wanted Beatles' records.

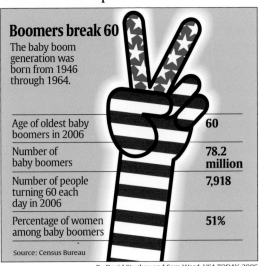

USA TODAY Snapshots®

Boomers break 60

The baby boom generation was born from 1946 through 1964.

Age of oldest baby boomers in 2006	**60**
Number of baby boomers	**78.2 million**
Number of people turning 60 each day in 2006	**7,918**
Percentage of women among baby boomers	**51%**

Source: Census Bureau

By David Stuckey and Sam Ward, USA TODAY, 2006

Spreading the mania: After the U.S. tour, Beatlemania spread throughout North America. These fans in Toronto, Canada, express their devotion in the usual way—with high-pitched screams.

The media, especially television, also played an important role in Beatlemania. Had The Beatles come on the scene a decade earlier, most people wouldn't have been able to see them outside of a live performance. Not all families owned televisions in the early 1950s, and program offerings were limited. But the *Ed Sullivan* broadcast carried The Beatles into millions of homes. Their performances were shared experiences for the whole nation. Everyone could talk about them the next day, since nearly everyone had seen them. Finally, Beatlemania fed more Beatlemania. Stories about fans going crazy in one place told fans in other places how they should act. Being a fan meant you could just go crazy. And they did.

Scene stealers: In a scene from their first movie, *A Hard Day's Night* (1964), the Fab Four sprint down an alley to escape screaming fans. The movie's title came from a malapropism (misused phrase) Ringo had said when he was tired.

A Hard Day's Night

No one noticed the old gentleman as he walked toward the crowd. They were too busy waiting for a glimpse of their heroes inside the television studio. The man tried to get their attention, but no one heard. Then he announced loudly that he had Beatles' pictures—signed by the Fab Four themselves. In an instant, young girls surrounded him, clamoring for the photos. He could have sold a thousand if he'd had them. Then again, he was lucky he wasn't simply run over by the desperate fans.

This scene wasn't real—it's actually from a movie, *A Hard Day's Night*, which The Beatles began filming after returning from the United States in February 1964. But the scene and the movie neatly summed up Beatlemania. The Beatles were in demand for everything and anything: concerts, albums, television shows, films, photos, magazines, dolls, lunch boxes, toys, and even lamps. Anything with their picture or simply their name on it sold. The world couldn't seem to get enough of them.

A Hard Day's Night made fun of Beatlemania. It featured a lot of Beatles' music and plenty of gags, sort of like a Marx Brothers movie or the rock mockumentary movie *This Is Spinal Tap* (1984), with music videos thrown in. The plot is simplistic—The Beatles play themselves on their way to a television performance. Girls chase the band members down the streets. They're admitted everywhere and forgiven everything. The film captures the zaniness that surrounded John, Paul, George, and Ringo in real life. The movie also hints at some of the work behind the fame: the many rehearsals, the boredom of traveling, and the temptations such as drinking and gambling. Directed by Richard

London premiere: The black-and-white *A Hard Day's Night* premiered in London in July 1964 to positive reviews. The sound track album of the same name came out soon afterward.

Lester, *A Hard Day's Night* was a big success when it was released in July 1964. So was its sound track album, which came out in August.

During the shooting of the film, George met Pattie Boyd, an actress with a minor role in the movie. They began dating and eventually married. At first, however, they kept their relationship as quiet as possible. Publicity about girlfriends would inter-

George and Pattie: Model and actress Pattie Boyd had a bit part in *A Hard Day's Night*, playing a schoolgirl. She caught George's eye, and they married a couple years later.

fere with female fans' fantasies about dating and marrying one of The Beatles. More than their image as eligible bachelors was at stake, however. Jealous fans were constantly harassing The Beatles' girlfriends and John's wife, Cynthia. Privacy was becoming more and more important to the band members—and more and more difficult to maintain.

"Can't Buy Me Love"

The *Hard Day's Night* sound track included a song called "Can't Buy Me Love." Instantly a Beatles' classic, the song reminds listeners that money isn't everything. That simple idea was an important one for The Beatles, who repeated it often. Many of their fans, young and idealistic, fervently agreed.

Not that The Beatles didn't care about money at all. It couldn't buy love, but it could buy a lot. And John, Paul, George, and Ringo suddenly had more money than they ever had before. John, for example, soon bought a Rolls-Royce, a Ferrari, and a Mini Cooper sports car.

Even so, The Beatles weren't rich. Before they were famous, they had agreed to perform concerts at relatively low rates. The record contract with Parlophone, signed when they were unknown, was also very stingy. And while companies were churning out everything from Beatles T-shirts to Beatles lamps, The Beatles themselves got very little payment from the use of their name. Although they eventually made new agreements with higher fees, the small cut rankled The Beatles. They saw that others were getting rich off their hard work.

Another deal that hurt The Beatles severely had to do with the ownership of their songs. John Lennon and Paul McCartney composed most of the early Beatles' songs. They made a deal with a small music publisher and formed a separate company called Northern Songs, which would own and publish all Lennon-McCartney songs. Unfortunately, the deal gave The Beatles and Brian Epstein only 49 percent of the company's shares. That meant they didn't control the company and they didn't fully own or control their songs.

The early songs could be used in advertisements without their permission, for example. What's more, a lot of the company's profits went not to Paul and John but to other shareholders. (Paul later spent many years trying to buy back the rights to his songs but never succeeded.)

Everything Beatles: Fans could buy virtually anything—including hair spray—with the faces of the Fab Four on the packaging.

Songs, like other creative works such as paintings and books, begin their life belonging to the person who created them. This person (or team, like Lennon and McCartney) has the right to "rent" them to others, collecting a fee called a royalty each time the song is used. Or the person can sell them to someone else, who can then collect the royalty.

Back to the United States

Before they were famous, The Beatles played as many gigs as they could. They did the same thing after they became famous, only for much larger audiences. In August 1964, they left Britain for a full tour of the United States. Starting in San Francisco, California, the band gave twenty-six shows in a little more than a month.

Hits like "Twist and Shout," "All My Loving," "She Loves You," "Can't Buy Me Love," "I Want to Hold Your Hand," "A Hard Day's Night," and Little Richard's "Long Tall Sally" were all standard parts of the shows on the U.S. tour. So was nearly non-stop screaming by teenage girls, who sometimes threw

USA TODAY Snapshots®

Yeah, yeah, yeah

Members of the Beatles, circa 1963, by Apple Corps Ltd.

How many times do the Beatles sing the word "yeah" in *She Loves You*?

Source: USA TODAY research   Answer: **29**

By Anne R. Carey and Julie Snider, USA TODAY, 2009

and waved underwear at the group. At least twice, berserk fans interrupted concerts.

At the Gator Bowl in Jacksonville, Florida, the promoter wanted black audience members separated from whites, a practice that was common in the American South at the time. The band refused to go on until their black fans were allowed to sit with the rest of the audience. To lure the band to play in Kansas City, Missouri, a businessman named Charles Finley paid them $150,000 up front, about six times their normal rate. Even their normal rate of $25,000 per show was unheard of for performers at the time.

When The Beatles got back to Britain, they began recording a new album and then started another British tour. While the places they played in were smaller than the American venues, the crowds were just as enthusiastic. Beatlemania was in full bloom.

Pushing the Limits

The songs in the standard Beatles' shows were familiar to the fans. They were mostly hits as singles. They fit in the line of traditional rock 'n' roll that The Beatles had played since their early Liverpool days.

The Beatles had given rock their own spin and accent, but their sound was still heavily influenced by earlier groups. In the recording studio, though, The Beatles' creativity took them in new directions. "She's a Woman," a song on the *Beatles for Sale* album, showed a strong blues influence. "Eight Days a Week," also on *Beatles for Sale*, began with a recording technique called a fade up, an unusual twist. On *Rubber Soul*, released in December 1965, "What Goes On" had a definite country-western feel. On the same album, "Nowhere Man" broke completely with usual pop song themes, telling the story of a man removed from normal life. The band's sound was evolving and expanding.

The Beatles took their musical experimentation even further with *Revolver*, released in 1966. One song on the album, "Eleanor Rigby," tells about a lonely old woman forgotten by society. In the future, other Beatles' songs would address serious topics such as peace and

IN FOCUS

Audio Technology

Modern computers make it possible to construct a record from many separate tracks, or recordings. Engineers can record each instrument or voice separately and can then manipulate the tracks in many ways. They can speed up or slow down the music. They can stop it and restart it. They can slice bits of music away. They can also synthesize, or create, a wide variety of sounds from scratch. They can combine different tracks in endless ways.

But none of these techniques was possible when The Beatles began making records. Instead, the entire group had to play and sing at once, and the whole performance was taped. If one band member made a mistake—or if the engineer goofed—everybody had to start again.

The technology for playing back recorded music was also very basic during the early 1960s. Surround sound and systems such as Dolby Digital were unheard of then. Most people listened to music on small radios or turntables. The equipment was monophonic, meaning that it played just one recorded track through a single speaker. Stereophonic equipment, which plays music from two tracks through two speakers, was still new when The Beatles began recording.

social justice. The Beatles showed that pop music could also make a political statement.

George Martin helped The Beatles arrange their music—figuring out the parts for each instrument and voice. As the producer, he also oversaw recording and engineering. He introduced techniques such as overdubbing, which involves using two tapes of the same vocal part to add depth to a recorded song. These techniques have since become standard in the music industry, but at the time, they were innovations.

The willingness to innovate and experiment made The Beatles truly different from the bands that had come before. Not only were they wildly successful, but they also continued to experiment. And their experiments were also wildly successful. Their popularity made it possible for them to try new creative techniques. Their musical abilities made the techniques they tried work.

Bigger Than God

During the summer of 1965, The Beatles were as popular as ever. Their songs dominated the pop charts throughout the world. When they arrived by helicopter in New York's Shea Stadium for a concert that summer, the screams of the crowd drowned out the roar of the helicopter's engines.

But fame had a dark side. Before and after performances, the band was mobbed and sometimes followed. When they weren't traveling or performing, John, Paul, George, and Ringo were often confined to their hotel rooms, prisoners of their own fame. Their image as lovable mop tops also felt like a straitjacket. They weren't supposed to

Shea Stadium: Normally the venue for baseball games, Shea Stadium in New York hosted what was up until then the largest single music concert. More than fifty-five thousand fans screamed from the stands as The Beatles performed on the playing field in August 1965.

Dressing up: The Beatles got away from their subdued suits and ties in the mid-1960s. John, who was severely near-sighted and wore glasses in private, even began wearing glasses in public—something he avoided doing in the early days of the band.

Highs and Lows

The typical American high school yearbook of 1962 or 1963 shows young men with close-cropped haircuts and suits and ties. Young women appear in dresses and skirts that fall below their knees, their hair carefully set. In even the most casual photographs of this era, students seem extremely careful, even stilted, in their appearance. Their clothes seem very formal.

Pick up a yearbook from five or six years later, and all the styles have changed. Many boys have hair below their ears, and in some cases, beyond their shoulders. Jeans are the most common item of clothing, worn by students of both sexes. Beads, wild colors, and casual clothes are the norm.

Fashions changed remarkably during the 1960s. The Beatles helped pave the way for some of these changes—long hair on boys, for example. But the dramatic changes in hair and fashion were only a small part of a whirlwind of change that shook society in the 1960s. Across the United States, young people challenged accepted ideas about sex, race, religion, careers, and women's roles in society. Long-haired hippies wore wild clothes and talked about peace and love. Many young people experimented with drugs. At speeches, marches, and demonstrations, many college students violently denounced U.S. involvement in the Vietnam War (1954–1975).

In many cases, the older generation resisted these changes. Discussions on a variety of topics—beginning with the length of boys' hair—pitted parents against teenagers in many households. Commentators called this division between young and old the generation gap.

The Beatles were at the center of this youthful rebellion, and they quickly took up the new styles themselves. In the mid-1960s, they stopped wearing their formal suits and began wearing psychedelic clothing, decorated with wild colors and unusual patterns. They grew their hair even longer than before and grew mustaches and beards. They began to experiment with illegal drugs and Eastern religions. John Lennon became an outspoken advocate of peace. Millions of young fans followed the band members' lead, experimenting with new ideas and new fashions.

Many young people rushed to buy wire-rimmed "granny glasses," just like those that John Lennon wore. The Beatles' popularity as rock stars made them extremely influential, even though they hadn't set out to be. In the few short years and many long, hard nights since their appearance on *The Ed Sullivan Show*, The Beatles had become role models for an entire generation.

On Top–and Beat

By late 1966, The Beatles were the most successful group in the history of pop music. Whether their achievements were measured in money, fame, or creative output, no one else came close. In four years, they had recorded and released seven LPs in Britain: *Please Please Me* (1963), *With The Beatles* (1963), *A Hard Day's Night* (1964), *Beatles for Sale* (1964), *Help!* (1965), *Rubber Soul* (1965), and *Revolver* (1966). Thirteen albums with mostly the same songs had been released in the United States. A dozen singles had gone to number one in Britain. Another dozen had topped the charts in the United States.

The Beatles had acted and played music in two movies, *A Hard Day's Night* (1964) and *Help!* (1965), a spoof of the popular James Bond hi-tech spy films. They had played around the world to sellout crowds. More people knew who they were than could be counted.

IN FOCUS

Scrambled Eggs

One of The Beatles' most successful songs ever was "Yesterday," a simple ballad sung and written by Paul. The words are haunting, a true testament to love.

Or to breakfast. Scrambled eggs, actually. Because the melody was written long before the words. It came to McCartney in a dream, and he just began playing it. Everyone loved the tune, but the only words Paul could put to it were "scrambled eggs, oh my baby, how I love your legs."

"There was generally a laugh at that point," said Paul. "You didn't need to do any more lyrics."

George Martin and the other Beatles urged him to do a little better. He kept playing with the tune during the filming of The Beatles' second movie, *Help!* Finally during a car ride, the words started to come.

Off tour: During the band's break from touring, John *(left)* acted in the 1967 movie *How I Won the War.* Ringo married his longtime girlfriend, Maureen Cox.

But The Beatles were also tired, exhausted by their years of hard work. Since the late 1950s, John, Paul, and George had been constant companions. Beatlemania locked them together on a never-ending roller coaster. They careened from studios to limos to concert halls to airplanes to hotel rooms and back around again. When their 1966 U.S. tour ended, they returned home and began their first long vacation away from one another.

George went to India with his wife, Pattie, to study Indian music. While there, they became interested in Indian spiritual beliefs. John joined the peace movement and took a supporting role in an antiwar film called *How I Won the War.* Living in London, Paul spent a lot of time with avant-garde artists who were exploring new concepts such as performance art. Ringo married his girlfriend, Maureen Cox, in February 1965. Their son, Zak, was born later that year. During the summer of 1966, they bought a house in London and fixed it up.

Going Home in Song

In late November 1966, The Beatles got back together in the studio. They began recording a new song written by John, "Strawberry Fields Forever," inspired by a real place near John's childhood home. A Salvation Army camp, Strawberry Field hosted flower shows each summer and concerts with music by the Salvation Army band. John tried to evoke the feeling of

Liverpool lyrics: Strawberry Field was near where John grew up in Liverpool. It became the basis of The Beatles song "Strawberry Fields Forever." Likewise, another song, "Penny Lane," was inspired by a busy shopping area in Liverpool.

those shows in his song. His words and music are like a lighthearted walk through a summer garden. In the studio, John and the other Beatles made the song into a kind of sound picture. They added orchestral music, sound effects such as cymbals recorded and played backward, and unusual instruments to more traditional vocal and musical styles.

Producer George Martin played an especially important role in recording this song. He helped construct the sound images. Even more important, he spliced together two completely different versions of the song. When Lennon suggested that George put the two takes together, Martin was dumbfounded. "They're in two different keys and they're also in different tempos," he protested. "I'm sure you can fix it," Lennon told him. Then he walked away.

Martin did fix it. He changed the speed on both recordings, bringing the keys and the tempos together. He then spliced the songs seamlessly together. "If you want to know where the two songs are actually joined," Martin said later, "it's exactly one minute in from the beginning."

"Strawberry Fields Forever" was like no other rock 'n' roll song ever produced. It relied heavily on recording technology as well as creativity. It also required a producer like George Martin—a person who could pull the complicated strands together. And it was only the beginning.

A Leap Beyond

The music and sound of "Strawberry Fields Forever" were radical, but the song's subject was a return home for John—he was writing about Liverpool and his childhood. His songwriting was gradually becoming more autobiographical. More and more, he wrote directly from his own experiences and feelings.

Another song, written by Paul and recorded around the same time, was also a return to Liverpool. It was "Penny Lane," named after a street in the city. While Paul changed a few details, the words paint an accurate picture of the Penny Lane area. Both Beatles seemed to be nostalgic for simpler times, even as they raced ahead.

The group planned the songs for a new album. But their record company wanted The Beatles to release a single, knowing it would be a hit. So the two songs were put back-to-back on a 45, released in February 1967. Critics and other musicians immediately realized that The Beatles were going in a new and exciting direction.

The group continued working on songs for a new album, and they wanted it to have a common theme. They had first intended to build the album around the returning home theme of "Strawberry Fields Forever" and "Penny Lane," but that idea fell by the wayside. Then Paul began writing a song called "Sgt. Pepper's Lonely Hearts Club Band." The Beatles were off in a new direction and never looked back.

"Just an ordinary song, not particularly brilliant as songs go," said George Martin. "When we'd finished it, Paul said, 'Why don't we make the whole album as though the Pepper Band really existed, as though Sgt. Pepper was doing the record. We can dub effects and things.' From that moment, it was as if Pepper had a life of its own."

All together now: The cover of the highly experimental 1967 album *Sgt. Pepper's Lonely Hearts Club Band* includes The Beatles in flashy silk band uniforms surrounded by pictures of famous and not-so-famous people.

This idea gave the album, also called *Sgt. Pepper's Lonely Hearts Club Band*, a loose theme—it was supposed to contain songs performed by a pretend pop band. Careful listening shows that the lyrics and music of the different songs don't have much in common. What they do share, however, is intense studio experimentation.

Sgt. Pepper was influenced by *Pet Sounds*, an album by the American group the Beach Boys. But *Sgt. Pepper* went far beyond *Pet Sounds* in its layering of music, pushing the edge of rock much further. George Martin and the engineers used many audio tricks, such as adding sound effects and slowing down or speeding up the tape to change the sound of a voice or an instrument. The album went beyond anything done in pop music before, and its huge commercial success led more musicians to experiment with new technology in the studio.

IN FOCUS

Beach Boys

While The Beatles inspired many musicians during the 1960s, they too were inspired by what others were doing. *Sgt. Pepper*, for example, might not have gone as far as it did without an album by the Beach Boys called *Pet Sounds*.

The Beach Boys were a California band that featured elaborate harmonies. Partly because of the subject matter of their songs and partly because of where they started, their music was known as the surf or California sound. The core of the group consisted of three brothers—Brian, Dennis, and Carl Wilson. They were joined by their cousin Mike Love and a friend, Al Jardine.

Pet Sounds was released in May 1966, before The Beatles began the *Sgt. Pepper* sessions. The album was much more elaborate than earlier Beach Boy albums. Brian Wilson recorded the instruments and basic tracks separately. He added special sounds to create a "feel" on some of the songs. After these basic tracks were complete, the rest of the group added the vocals.

Beach Boys: The California band had a distinctive, harmonious sound. They also began experimenting with different studio techniques during the mid-1960s.

Lucy in the Sky

One of the album's most famous songs was "Lucy in the Sky with Diamonds." The music starts slowly, then careens wildly. The lyrics seem
fantastical. The strange sounds and lyrics and the initials of the main
words in the title—*LSD*—seemed to refer to the mind-altering drug
LSD. Many young people, including The Beatles, were experimenting
with this drug at the time. Many listeners concluded that the song
celebrated drugs and was based on a drug trip.

John actually began writing the song by describing a picture
drawn by his young son, Julian. The picture, Paul explained, showed
a girl floating in the sky with diamonds. "He played me the idea he
had for it, starting with 'Picture yourself,'" Paul told George Martin
later. "We discussed Lewis Carroll and the Alice [in Wonderland]
books and how this title would make a great psychedelic song. We
began to trade images with each other. I sug-
gested 'cellophane flow-
ers.' . . . John countered
with 'the girl with kalei-
doscope eyes.'" Paul said
the LSD connection was
something they realized
only later.

Other songs on the
album included "A Day
in the Life," "With a
Little Help from My
Friends," and "When I'm
Sixty-Four," a song Paul
wrote for his father's six-
ty-fourth birthday. The

John and Julian: A picture that John's son
Julian drew when he was little inspired the song
"Lucy in the Sky with Diamonds."

www.usatoday.com

USA TODAY

News

SECTION A

May 29, 1987

It Was 20 Years Ago Today

From the Pages of **USA TODAY**

Rock's most celebrated album reaches stores in compact disc form on Monday—20 years to the day since The Beatles' historic LP was released in Britain. For millions, *Sgt. Pepper* became a '60s soundtrack and the theme music for a rebellious generation's groovy coming-out party. Today, it remains an indelible musical and cultural totem of its time, in which The Beatles ushered in state-of-the-art rock by donning the costumes of an old-time oom-pah band.

The album sold 2½ million copies that summer alone, and its watershed success compounded the already enormous influence of The Beatles. "They were among those select few who became far more powerful than they wanted to be or could even conceive of being," says rock impresario Bill Graham, who was promoting concerts at San Francisco's Fillmore Auditorium when *Sgt. Pepper* hit the streets. "They realized they had a seductive power and a leadership role. They were among the involuntary leaders of that whole new society, and the release of that album just magnified that role."

It was the first pop record to receive, if not demand, treatment as a work of art. From its richly produced performances that demanded headphones, to its whimsically elaborate cover, *Sgt. Pepper* revolutionized pop records. "It changed music. Creatively, it was just light-years ahead of everything," says rock 'n' roll crooner Dion DiMucci, pictured in the *Sgt. Pepper* album cover's famous background photo montage with the likes of Marilyn Monroe, Edgar Allan Poe, Shirley Temple, and other luminaries.

Long after the thunderous 45-second piano chord ending of the album's climactic "A Day in the Life" first faded, the influence of *Sgt. Pepper* remains. Though many fans prefer other classic Beatles LPs such as *Rubber Soul* or *Revolver*, it remained the top pick of critics and broadcasters in Paul Gambaccini's book, *The Top 100 Rock 'n' Roll Albums*.

The album's first and last lyrics were appropriate bookends: "It was twenty years ago today, Sgt. Pepper taught the band to play," McCartney began. "I'd love to turn you on," Lennon ended. On *Sgt. Pepper*, The Beatles did both.

—John Milward and Patrick O'Driscoll

album cost twenty-five thousand pounds to make—a huge sum for a rock album in 1967 and about twenty times what the first Beatles' album had cost to produce. It took nearly five months to complete. It was The Beatles' riskiest and most expensive album ever. It was an immediate smash.

An Unhappy Success

Brian Epstein had been critical to The Beatles' success. Besides managing The Beatles, he also managed other musical groups and ran a successful management company, NEMS. He owned a large portion of a London theater. With two homes and a great deal of wealth, he was by most definitions successful.

But he was also unhappy and under a great deal of stress. He may have been worried about his future with The Beatles, since his contract with them was due to run out in 1967. He was in no danger of being replaced, but if the group didn't tour, his role would be less important. At some point, Epstein began taking sleeping pills. He also drank heavily and occasionally used other drugs, including amphetamines. At times his drug use was out of control.

On the weekend of August 25, 1967, all four Beatles traveled by train to Bangor, Wales, to meet an Indian spiritual teacher named Maharishi Mahesh Yogi. He was teaching transcendental meditation, an Eastern meditation technique. George, who had visited India the year before, introduced Indian spiritual practices to the other Beatles. On the spur of the moment, they decided to visit the Maharishi and learn firsthand about his beliefs. Several friends, including Mick Jagger of the Rolling Stones, traveled with them.

Brian Epstein was invited to join them over the weekend. He never showed. On Sunday afternoon, the band members got a call saying that Brian had been found dead in his London apartment. An investigation showed that he had died from an accidental overdose of sleeping pills.

Shaken, The Beatles returned to London. *Sgt. Pepper* had shattered the early Beatles' image as lovable mop tops. The album's music took

Loss of Brian: The Beatles had come to rely on Brian Epstein *(far left)* to handle their business details. His death was hard for the band to deal with.

them far beyond their rock roots. With Brian Epstein's death, they were about to enter a new phase in their business careers as well.

A New Phase

Before Brian Epstein's death, The Beatles had planned to create a new company to coordinate their business interests. With Epstein's death, this company became much more important and the band members took a more direct role in it than previously planned.

The company was called Apple Corps, or simply Apple. It would be the "core" of their operation, managing their record releases, films, and other creative projects. The company would have a record division to produce other artists' music. An Apple Boutique would sell clothes and other items. A division called Apple Films would release movies.

"It's a business concerning records, films, and electronics and, as a sideline, manufacturing or whatever," explained John at a press conference announcing Apple. "We want to set up a system whereby people who just want to make a film about anything don't have to go on their knees in somebody's office [beg a producer]."

The Beatles wanted Apple to be less greedy and more democratic than other companies. They wanted the busi-

New business: The logo for The Beatles new venture, Apple Corps, was a bright, shiny, green apple.

ness to be fun, explained Peter Brown, a longtime Beatles associate and the company's administrative director. But managing the money and business details of the band was complicated. Individual Beatles had different ideas about how the company should operate, and these differences led to conflicts. The British government also took a high percentage of their income in taxes, which put further strain on the group.

As the band's manager, Brian Epstein had overseen all of their business arrangements. "When Brian Epstein was alive," explained Epstein's biographer, Ray Coleman, "nothing went wrong for The Beatles; when he died, little went right for them outside of music." Coleman explained that Brian had allowed The Beatles to do what they did best—make music. With Apple, the band members were soon in unfamiliar territory.

A Film Flop

In September 1967, The Beatles began filming a movie called *Magical Mystery Tour*. Conceived mostly by Paul, the film was supposed to represent a psychedelic trip—sort of the movie equivalent of the *Sgt. Pepper* music. The film showed The Beatles and friends boarding a bus and wandering around the countryside. Their fantasy experiences would be as important as the real places they visited.

The songs that were part of the film, including "The Fool on the Hill" and "I Am the Walrus," continued the experiments and recording techniques used with *Sgt. Pepper*. Many of the songs quickly became classics. The film, however, was chaotic and uneven. Broadcast on TV by the British Broadcasting Corporation [BBC] around Christmas, the film flopped.

Happy enough: The band looked relaxed during a break in the filming of *Magical Mystery Tour* in 1967.

Many people attacked the movie, claiming it advocated drug use. Others criticized its disjointed and experimental style. "If they were not The Beatles, the BBC would not have fallen for it," said the *London Daily Mirror*. "Beatles bomb with Yule [Christmastime] film," said the *Los Angeles Times*. The film was never shown in the United States, even though the album quickly topped the charts.

CHAPTER SIX

Yoko and the band: After John hooked up with Yoko Ono in 1968, the couple spent nearly every hour together. Yoko was in the recording studio while The Beatles practiced and rehearsed their albums.

Crash

John Lennon, bemused and a little confused, climbed up a stepladder. Above his head was a piece of canvas. A small spyglass, or telescope, was suspended from a chain. When he reached the top of the ladder, Lennon put his eye to the spyglass. He maneuvered the glass toward the canvas, aligning it to read a message, a single word in capital letters: *YES.*

Yes.

Yes? Was it art? Or something else?

Yes.

Lennon was visiting an art show at the Indica Gallery in London. The ladder hadn't been left by a worker. It was part of a show prepared by Yoko Ono, an avant-garde American artist. The show featured odd items, including a bag of nails, and an apple with a two-hundred pound ($480) price tag.

"You're on this ladder," Lennon told an interviewer years later, "you feel like a fool, you could fall any minute—and you look through it and it just says 'YES.' Well, all the so-called avant-garde art at the time, and everything that was supposedly interesting, was all . . . boring, negative crap. It was all anti-, anti-, anti-. Anti-art, anti-establishment. And just that 'YES' made me stay in a gallery full of apples and nails instead of just walking out."

New Loves

Seven years older than Lennon and married to her second husband, Yoko Ono seems to have fallen in love with John Lennon from the moment they were introduced at the show in late 1966. John had been married for several years, but Yoko sent him cryptic notes and managed to stay in touch. Although John had lost interest in his marriage, he wasn't attracted to Yoko at first. He did, however, provide funding for another exhibit of Yoko's work. And he gradually grew more interested in her as well as her art.

In May 1968, while Cynthia was away in Greece, John invited Yoko to come listen to some avant-garde music he was creating in his basement studio. When Cynthia returned from her vacation, she found Yoko and John in their bathrobes having breakfast. Within a few weeks, John and Yoko were inseparable.

Paul McCartney's love life also changed around this time. In May 1967, at a press reception for *Sgt. Pepper* in London, he met a young American photographer named Linda Eastman. A divorced mother, Linda had recently made a name for herself photographing rock stars. She was tall, intelligent, and good-looking, with long blonde hair and a self-assured manner. Her father was a well-known attorney in New York City, with many clients in the entertainment industry. The following

Paul and Linda: Paul and Linda Eastman *(right)* are deep in conversation at a press conference for the release of *Sgt. Pepper*. They married in 1969.

year, Paul and Linda ran into each other again in the United States. Soon they began dating. The relationship flourished, and they later married. (Paul adopted Linda's daughter, and the couple eventually would have three children together. One of their daughters, Stella McCartney, is a well-known fashion designer.)

The White Album

The Beatles' search for spiritual guidance took them to India in early 1968, again to study with the Maharishi Mahesh Yogi. Ringo left India after two weeks, when he and his wife got homesick, but the others stayed and studied meditation and other spiritual practices. They stopped eating meat and all became lifelong vegetarians. They also continued to write songs, finishing forty while they were there. "It was really very interesting and I will continue to meditate," Paul said, when he decided to leave India after five weeks.

John and George stayed on for two more weeks, but they began to grow disenchanted with their spiritual teacher. John especially began

Meditation helps focus the mind through quiet periods of deep concentration. Different forms of meditation, from silent prayers to group chanting, are used in religious and spiritual practices. Transcendental Meditation, which is what the Maharishi Mahesh Yogi taught The Beatles, has its own special techniques for focusing the mind.

to doubt that the Maharishi had any real answers about life. Finally, after rumors that the religious leader was having an affair with one of the other students, John and George left too.

The Beatles began recording in the summer of 1968, after their return from India. The album once again broke new ground—in part because of its music but more because it featured The Beatles as individual musicians rather than a group. The band members worked more independently on songs than ever before. John, Paul, and George each created some tracks almost singlehandedly, with little help from the others.

Although it was officially called *The Beatles*, fans called the records the White Album because the cover was pure white, with only the words *The Beatles* printed on the front. It was the first two-record set for the group. The album showed off the wide range of The Beatles' songwriting interests. Like those on *Sgt. Pepper* and *Magical Mystery Tour*, the tracks were constructed with overdubs, sound effects, and various instruments. But the album also contained straightforward rockers that updated the group's early sound.

Among these songs was "Back in the U.S.S.R." Written by Paul in India, the song is a takeoff of an early Chuck Berry tune, "Back in the U.S.A." The song also contains a tribute to and parody of the Beach Boys. Mostly known for their surfing songs and tight harmonies, the group had always been considered a serious competitor to The Beatles.

In this track, The Beatles showed they could master the California surf sound that the Beach Boys had popularized.

"Revolution 1," written by John, has The Beatles playing heavy guitar riffs. The words express John's political philosophy, encouraging peaceful change to make the world better. Paul's "Ob-La-Di, Ob-La-Da" features a playful, easygoing rhythm. So does John's "The Continuing Story of Bungalow Bill," but its lyrics are more complex. In this song, Lennon uses irony to put forth an antigun and antihunter message. George Harrison wrote several songs for the album, including one of his best-known compositions, "While My Guitar Gently Weeps." The song featured the guitar playing of George's friend Eric Clapton, who was becoming a rock icon in his own right when the recording was made.

One of the Beatles best-known love songs, "Something," was written by George Harrison. It is said to have been written for his wife at the time, Pattie.

The most controversial song on the album is "Revolution 9," which is more of a sound collage than a song. It contains orchestral music, seemingly random voices, and bits of jumbled sound effects that all seem to run together in a sometimes melodic, sometimes maddening flow. The piece has a definite movement, but it doesn't sound like a traditional rock or pop song.

Conflict

George Martin felt that some of the material on the White Album should have been left out. He felt that a single album would have been stronger than a double one. On the other hand, releasing a double album let The Beatles express a wide range of musical styles. It may also have helped them avoid arguments about whose material to use. For the first time in their history, differences in personalities and musical interests were causing serious creative conflicts.

At first, the differences seemed petty, at least when viewed from a distance. John was upset because Paul didn't ask him to work on a song he liked. The others called Paul too much of a perfectionist. At one point, Ringo quit the sessions, saying he was leaving the band. But he returned after two weeks.

Yoko Ono was another source of irritation. During the recording for the White Album, she sat in on the sessions. She perched on the band's monitor speakers, which irked Paul. She also whispered to John and offered advice to the others, which they clearly did not want. From Paul's point of view, she was an interfering know-it-all, out for John's money and fame. And she knew nothing about rock 'n' roll, the other Beatles said. Eventually, everything she did bothered someone.

Yoko had become a kind of muse, or inspiration, to John, but there were other reasons he wanted her close to him that summer. Yoko was pregnant, and he was concerned about her health. (She suffered a miscarriage in November 1968.) Above all, John's relationship with Yoko was a deep one, far more important to him than his marriage to Cynthia. "I'm JOHNANDYOKO" he would write and say many times.

John resented the group's attitude toward Yoko. He and Yoko soon divorced their spouses and married each other in Gibraltar, a British colony connected to Spain, in 1969. John's song "The Ballad of John and Yoko" recounts the wedding.

One bright spot for The Beatles in 1968 was the release of a third Beatles' movie, *Yellow Submarine*. A full-length animated feature, it instantly became a hit. Directed by George Dunning, the movie has a light plot inspired by The Beatles' song of the same name, part of the 1966 *Revolver* album. In the movie, cartoon Beatles battle the Blue Meanies, making the seas safe for civilization—or at least rock 'n' roll.

The band members actually had little to do with the project. Other actors provided the voices for their cartoon characters, and the band recorded only a few songs for the movie. The sound track album included

Yellow Submarine: The animated film *Yellow Submarine* (1968) was based on a song Ringo sang on *Revolver*.

an entire side of instrumentals arranged by George Martin. The music did not match the standards of The Beatles' other albums. Even so, the movie was well received and helped boost The Beatles' popularity.

But not much else was going right for The Beatles. Their friendships were clearly strained, and the situation soon got much worse. Apple Corps, the company set up to manage the band's business affairs, was supposed to be as revolutionary as The Beatles' music. But it quickly became a mess. The Apple Boutique was perhaps the worst example. It opened on December 7, 1967, in a renovated building on Baker Street in London. The renovation itself had been chaotic, with the different Beatles ordering different construction work on whim.

Once the store opened, the situation quickly turned sour. Shoplifting was rampant. "Garments began rapidly to leave the premises, though seldom as a result of cash transactions," writes Beatles' biographer Philip Norman. The losses were immense. Finally, on July 30, 1968, the boutique ended its chaotic existence by giving away all of its merchandise.

May 11, 1999

Beatles all together now on lost song

From the Pages of
USA TODAY An unreleased song recorded at Abbey Road Studios during the *Yellow Submarine* sessions will come out in early September, along with retooled versions of the album and animated fantasy movie. "It is a rock-y song that lends itself to being a single," says Beatles spokesman Geoff Baker, declining to divulge the title. "It's a little gem, but that's all I can say right now."

The track is expected to reignite global Beatles fervor, ideal bait for the 30th anniversary relaunching of 1969's *Yellow Submarine*. The soundtrack, "completely different from the original," will contain additional previously released tracks and be the first Beatles album to undergo remixing, Baker says.

—Edna Gundersen

Apple Corps continued on, however. The part of the company that made records had several successes with performers besides The Beatles, including singer James Taylor. But for the most part, the business was out of control. Employees took advantage of free alcohol and practically nonstop parties—all funded by The Beatles. Hippies and Hells Angels (members of a rough motorcycle gang) roamed the halls.

When the band members set up the company, they had each agreed to give all of their earnings to the business for ten years. "If Apple goes on at this rate," John told a journalist in 1969, "we'll be broke in six months." He calculated the losses at twenty thousand pounds a week. In modern U.S. money, that figure would amount to millions of dollars a year.

Rockin' the roof: On top of Apple headquarters in London, The Beatles performed some new material at a lunchtime concert in January 1969.

The End of the Road

On January 30, 1969, the cold London air began jangling with something no fan had heard for nearly three years: The Beatles together, live, whipping through the chords of a fresh composition. With Paul in sneakers and John wearing a woman's mink coat, the group "made show" in central London. On a makeshift stage atop the Apple headquarters building, they tried out songs intended for a new album. For the next forty minutes or so, the lunchtime crowd received a free, traffic-stopping rehearsal and concert.

The session began and ended with "Get Back," a song that seemed to symbolize the entire project. The hard-driving beat harkened back to The Beatles' earliest roots. The planned album and a film that would accompany it were supposed to take The Beatles back to the spirit of their Hamburg days. The songs would be recorded live and would be released that way, mistakes and all. There would be no overdubbing. If John's fingers were too cold to play the chords right—as he complained following one song—that was just the way it was.

The London police brought the rooftop session to a premature end. It was a symbolic end to the Get Back project as well, though The Beatles struggled on for a few more sessions.

"The Low of All Time"

Because the Get Back project included a movie, much of the recording sessions were captured on film. The film shows a great deal of creativity on the part of band members but almost as much bickering and bad feelings. The band members couldn't decide how the songs should be played. At different times, they wondered if they should bother with the project at all. "It was the low of all time," said George Harrison later. "The most miserable sessions on earth," noted John. At one point, the two friends traded angry punches. The project was soon scrapped.

Part of the problem had to do with being rusty. The Beatles prided themselves on polished performances and tight shows. But they hadn't performed as a complete band in a long time. They had learned to work independently in the studio and had lost the feel for one another. Even when they tried to pull off an update of "Love Me Do," they couldn't get it together.

As Beatles' chronicler Mark Lewisohn wrote, "Although the Get Back project was supposed to be capturing The Beatles' rough edges, this recording was just too rough to be released." Two songs—"Get Back" and "Don't Let Me Down"—were culled for a single. The rest of the sessions remained on tape. Finally, more than a year later, they were heavily edited, remixed, and released as the album *Let It Be*.

The cause of The Beatles' problems in 1968 and 1969 was a combination of old and new strains. Apple and the chaos that surrounded it put incredible pressure on them. Paul and the others clashed over who to hire to run the firm. Northern Songs, the company John and Paul originally formed to publish their music, slipped completely out of their control in a complicated series of business maneuvers. Not owning the publishing rights to the songs they wrote was galling and frustrating.

 The publishing rights to most of The Beatles' 1960s catalog of songs eventually were bought by music icon Michael Jackson. The songwriters, however, still received 50 percent of the royalties from any rights sales.

In the past, Brian Epstein had buffered the band members from business pressures and problems. He had also acted as peacemaker. Without him, the pull toward individual interests was much stronger.

The Beatles' use of drugs was also a strain. John used LSD, heroin, and other drugs during the late 1960s. As a result, his actions at times were erratic. He was arrested in 1968 for possession of marijuana. He eventually pleaded guilty to the charge and received a small fine. George Harrison was also arrested for drug possession after a raid on his home in Esher, England. Both George and his wife pleaded guilty to possession and were fined as well.

Most of all, creativity worked to push The Beatles apart. While remaining as prolific as ever, the band members were growing in different directions. They wanted to explore new music and new interests—but not all of these interests were shared by the others. Record albums could hold only a limited number of songs, so band members had to compromise. Collaborating had helped spark their creative genius. But it also constrained them.

Strains and pains: George *(left)* and John *(right)* on guitar accompany Paul on the piano in a rehearsal of "Let It Be," a song from a later album of the same name. The group was fast losing the camaraderie that had long characterized their recording sessions.

George Harrison, who was blossoming as a songwriter, felt especially held back. He complained that he had written many songs worth recording that the others wouldn't even consider. In some ways, John and Paul treated him like a younger brother, not quite ready to play with the big boys. But that was nothing compared to how they treated each other. Their sessions were marked by bitterness and frustration. John had no patience for Paul's songs and music. Paul thought John was steering too far from melody. One of the greatest songwriting teams in the history of music now rarely agreed on anything.

The experience of playing and struggling together in the early days had welded The Beatles together. The bond was about more than just music. They were friends. As the disputes boiled over, the friendship at the center of The Beatles disintegrated. When it was gone, all that was left were four very talented individuals.

Abbey Road

The Get Back project had been a disaster. The idea of playing live wouldn't work—The Beatles were not a live band anymore. But they were still The Beatles, and they still had plenty of songs they wanted to record. So they went to work on another batch. They worked separately on many of the tracks, much as they had on the White Album. The result was *Abbey Road*, which many critics rank as The Beatles' greatest album. It contained many songs that became instant classics.

George Harrison's "Something," for example, may be one of the best-loved songs of all time. "Come Together," written by John Lennon, is a hard-edged rocker that incorporates experimental sounds into

George blossoms: George's songwriting skills finally were showcased on the *Abbey Road* album.

Abbey Road Studios

Although many rock 'n' roll bands recorded at the Abbey Road Studios from the 1960s to the 1990s, The Beatles made it famous. Naming their 1969 album *Abbey Road*, the cover featured a photo of John, Paul, Ringo, and George striding along the white painted crosswalk in front of the studios. From then on, the studio became a famous tourist stop for Beatle fans.

When rock 'n' roll was young, recording equipment was large and complicated to run. Bands needed to rent studio space and hire professional sound engineers who knew how to run the equipment. Once digital technology was invented,

Abbey Road: The London studio where The Beatles recorded was saved from being torn down, and is a National Trust historic museum.

musicians could record their songs on a personal computer in their own home. They didn't need expensive studios anymore.

a pop anthem. Paul McCartney seemed to go back to his fifties rock roots with "Oh! Darling." John and George influenced a generation or two of heavy metal rockers with the overlaid guitars on "I Want You (She's So Heavy)."

George Martin pointed out that the album's two sides have two different sounds. The first side is more stripped-down rock 'n' roll—the sound John wanted. "He wanted to get back to what he called 'honesty' in recording," said Martin. On the second side, the songs blend together like a symphonic suite—Paul's preference. John and Paul worked on songs on both sides of the album, but they were clearly going in different creative directions.

January 31, 2008

Beatles have ticket to ride to deep space

From the Pages of USA TODAY

Now *this* is a magical mystery tour. NASA has been beaming songs to astronauts since 1965 ... but for the first time, the agency will be sending a tune to deep space.... *Across the Universe* will travel across the universe. It's part of NASA's year-long 50th anniversary celebration and also marks exactly 40 years since The Beatles recorded the song [in 1968]. The Fab Four and NASA share a cozy history. *Here Comes the Sun*, *Ticket to Ride* and *A Hard Day's Night* have been transmitted as wake-up calls to astronauts, and Paul McCartney was the first person whose live music was relayed into space (his *Good Day Sunshine* was routed to the International Space Station in 2005). Informed of NASA's plans, McCartney sent a message: "Amazing! Well done, NASA! Send my love to the aliens."

—Edna Gundersen and Gary Strauss

The album was a great success, but the band members felt that something was missing. Friction between them had hurt not just the group but also the record, Paul said. "On *Abbey Road*, we don't do harmonies like we used to," he commented. "I think it's sad. On "Come Together," I would have liked to sing harmony with John, and I think he would have liked me to, but I was too embarrassed to ask him." In short, The Beatles would never "come together" as The Beatles again.

In September John accepted an invitation to appear at a rock revival show in Canada. While he and Yoko had already performed in public without The Beatles, their music was experimental. The Toronto

Breaking out: John and Yoko perform together at a concert in Toronto in 1969. John's willingness to be onstage separate from the other Beatles signaled that the band's breakup was near.

show was rock, and it was the first time a Beatle had performed at a major concert without The Beatles. After wailing through the numbers, Lennon came to the conclusion that had been inevitable for quite some time—The Beatles were over. "I might as well tell you, I'm leaving the group. I've had enough. I want a divorce, like my divorce from Cynthia," he told the others after he got back.

Paul wanted the group to continue. He kept pressing for a Beatles' live performance. George complained bitterly that the other two hadn't included his songs on their recent albums. The three longtime friends blew up at one another. As far as John was concerned, The Beatles had ceased to exist as a working band. But for business reasons, he agreed to keep quiet about his decision to leave the group. No one spoke publicly about the breakup. To the outside world at least, The Beatles were still The Beatles.

It was Paul, not John, who made the break official. He retreated to his Scottish farm in the winter of 1969–1970. He and his wife, Linda, laid down the tracks for a solo album there. It was a true solo album, since Paul played all the instruments. Still, he seems to have hoped the group would remain together.

On the farm: Paul bought High Park Farm in an isolated area of southwestern Scotland in 1968. When the band was going sour, he and Linda went to the farm to recover from the sadness of The Beatles' split.

But while he was working on his songs, Paul received a preview of *Let It Be*, the album created from the Get Back project. He was stunned. His song "The Long and Winding Road" had been meant as a simple ballad. He had recorded it that way. But The Beatles' new producer, Phil Spector, added violins, horns, and a choir to the final version. Furious, McCartney demanded that his version be restored, but it was not. Paul McCartney had lost creative control of his music. The end of The Beatles had truly come.

Paul Is Dead?

Of all the rumors involving The Beatles, the strangest was that Paul was dead. Millions of fans believed it. Disc jockeys repeated it. So-called experts proclaimed they had found clues that his voice wasn't on the albums.

Among the clues was the fact that Paul had his back to the camera on the back of the *Sgt. Pepper* cover. On *Magical Mystery Tour,* he had a black carnation. He didn't have any shoes on the *Abbey Road* cover. People said this meant Paul was a dead corpse, with John dressed as the preacher in a white suit, Ringo

the undertaker in black, and George, dressed in jeans, as the grave digger. The rumors reached a frenzy in the fall of 1969. A language and linguistic professor supposedly tested Beatles' records and found "reasonable doubt" that McCartney had recorded some songs.

Of course, McCartney was alive. He had been staying at his farm in Scotland, recording a solo album. "I am alive and well and unconcerned about the rumors of my death," he said in a press release. "But if I were dead, I would be the last to know."

John, Yoko, and Sean: John plays guitar for his son Sean, while Yoko looks on, in their New York City apartment in the late 1970s.

Afterlife

The Beatles forged ahead in their new careers, but their breakup did not end their financial problems. At one point, Paul sued the group in an attempt to dismantle The Beatles' partnership. He didn't trust Allen Klein, whom the other Beatles had hired to manage their affairs after Brian Epstein's death. Their ten-year legal battle brought new headaches and conflicts, but eventually tempers mellowed.

Even after their breakup, new records were released, including two double-album greatest hits collections and a host of "best" collections, live albums, and lesser-known recordings. Bootlegs (illegal recordings) appeared. A Broadway musical called *Beatlemania* premiered in 1977 and ran until 1979. It tried to capture the excitement and sound of the Fab Four. Rumors of a reunion of the band popped up now and again. Fate—and a deranged man—stepped in to end that hope.

Beyond Shock

It was warm for December. John Lennon and Yoko Ono told the limo driver to stop outside of the arched entrance to the Dakota, where they had their apartment in New York City. They liked to walk the last few steps to the building. Sometimes a few fans waited between the gate and the building to greet Lennon, but Beatlemania was long gone. It was 1980, and The Beatles had long since broken up. John Lennon was still famous, but he could usually walk around New York without being hounded or hassled.

John and Yoko were returning from a studio session that day, December 8. John carried the tapes from the session with him. They held a good piece of work—a song by Yoko for a new album. The couple had collaborated on a number of albums, and their latest one, *Double Fantasy*, had just come out. Critics said it was one of the best albums Lennon had ever worked on. Observers also noted that he seemed to have found a new peace to go along with his creative energy and ability.

Perhaps he had. In the decade since The Beatles had split up, John Lennon had passed through tumultuous times. First, he kicked a severe drug habit and a drinking problem. Then he split with Yoko. Eventually, the couple reunited, and their love grew stronger than ever. They had a son, Sean, and John devoted himself to raising him. For a while, he called himself a househusband. It was unusual at the time for a man to serve as an infant's primary caregiver, but John had a nurturing side—the opposite of the brash-talking rebel. He had also begun to repair his relationship with his older son, Julian, who was an aspiring musician with his own band.

Of course, John Lennon hadn't given up making music. An early post-Beatles' song, "Imagine," became as well known as anything he'd done with the band. He also played with hundreds of different musicians over the decade. Indeed, he had finally found peace after many hectic years.

Anniversary of death: Fans put flowers and memorabilia on the "Imagine" memorial in the Strawberry Fields section of New York City's Central Park in 2005 to commemorate the twenty-fifth anniversary of John's death.

John got out of the car and began striding through the gate toward the Dakota's front steps. "Mr. Lennon?" shouted a man.

John Lennon turned around to see who was calling him. As he did, the man pumped five bullets into his back and arm.

Mortally wounded, Lennon stumbled into the Dakota. "I'm shot, I'm shot," he told the man at the front desk as he fell to the floor. Within hours, he was dead.

John's death shocked the world and saddened millions of fans. But the event also drew people together. It seemed as if there were as many Beatles fans as ever.

Lennon's killer was a mentally disturbed man named Mark David Chapman. He was found guilty of murder and sentenced to twenty years to life in prison. His efforts to win parole have been unsuccessful.

The Fab Four Live On

The Beatles all had successful solo careers in the decades following the band's demise. And over time, animosities and anger died down, especially after John died.

Paul McCartney, with and without his band, Wings, continued to be a force in pop music. He made dozens of albums, including *McCartney*, his first solo effort, and *Wings over America*, released in 1976. He wrote film songs for *Live and Let Die* in 1973, *Spies Like Us* in 1985, *Vanilla Sky* in 2001, and *Everybody's Fine* in 2009.

Paul also continued to tour around the world, even returning to play at The Beatles old club, the Cavern in Liverpool, in December of 1999.

Still touring: Paul continues to thrill crowds on tour, singing a combination of old Beatles' tunes and songs he's written since the breakup.

USA TODAY
Life
SECTION D

December 16, 1999

McCartney gets back to Cavern

<u>From the Pages of</u>
<u>USA TODAY</u>

Paul McCartney's raucous return to the Cavern Club was a 47-minute express trip to the 1950s, with songs that reveled in the major keys of A, D and G. Most of the 13 tunes came from his latest album, *Run Devil Run*, a tribute to the American-bred music that inspired a legendary career. The exceptions included early Beatles standard "I Saw Her Standing There" and Eddie Cochran's "Twenty Flight Rock," a mul-tiverse ditty that McCartney described as the song that got him into The Beatles. "I knew all the words, so John said, 'OK, you're in,'" he joked from the tiny stage.

The old Cavern Club was a former fruit-and-vegetable cellar where McCartney played 280 times between 1958 and 1963, first with The Quarry-men, then with The Beatles. It was paved over in the '70s and rebuilt after Lennon's 1980 death. The gig was held in a modern room next to a re-creation of the original. Lyrics were punctuated with winks and raised eyebrows. Bass notes thundered unerringly. The Cute One's vocals were deep and Presleyesque on tunes such as "Blue Jean Bop," high and Beatlesque on "Try Not to Cry" and "Shake a Hand."

At the Cavern: Paul went back to perform at the Cavern in 1999. The last time he'd played there was in 1963 with The Beatles.

McCartney's fabled wit also has not dulled. Faced with fans screaming for favorites at breaks, he deadpanned: "Sorry. Don't do requests."

—Marco R. della Cava

In 2010 he headlined the first concert at the new Mets Citi Field in New York City, which replaced the original Shea Stadium where The Beatles had played to screaming fans in 1965.

Paul's won many awards and honors, including a knighthood in 1997 from Queen Elizabeth II, making him Sir Paul McCartney. He accepted the honor "on behalf of all the people of Liverpool and the other Beatles, without whom it wouldn't have been possible." In June 2010, Paul became the first British musician to win the Gershwin Prize, given to musicians whose work continues the tradition of legendary American songwriting brothers George and Ira Gershwin.

After The Beatles broke up, George Harrison blossomed as a singer, songwriter, and a producer. His first solo album, *All Things Must Pass*, was released to critical acclaim in 1970, followed by *The Concert for*

George rocks: After the breakup, George found his stride as a singer and a songwriter. He also moved into producing the records of other performers.

Olivia and George: George married Olivia Arias in 1978. She worked in the U.S. office of A&M Records, a recording company where George had a contract.

Bangladesh in 1971. He produced many records for other artists. Starting in the late 1980s, he joined Bob Dylan, Tom Petty, and Roy Orbison touring as the Traveling Wilburys. He wrote an autobiography, *I, Me, Mine,* in 1980.

George's interests continued to vary beyond music. He became a Formula One fan and was able to indulge his love of cars and racing. He took up gardening and turned his estate, Friar Park in Henley-on-Thames, into a showcase. He also fitted out a room with a state-of-the-art recording studio that rivaled the one at Abbey Road. His marriage to Pattie Boyd dissolved in 1974, and he married Olivia Arias in 1978.

Ringo Starr's post-Beatles career included a number of acting roles, as well as expanding into photography and painting. He had always preferred playing live to recording in a studio. But in addition to touring, he also produced more than a dozen albums, starting with a 1975 top-ten hit with "You're Sixteen." In 2009, nearing the age of seventy, his fifteenth album, *Y Not*, came out. It included two songs on which Paul collaborated.

January 13, 2010

Ringo turning the big 7-0

<u>From the Pages of</u>
<u>USA TODAY</u>
The age bearing down on Beatledom this year is 70. Boomers may wince, but Ringo the eldest hits that milestone on July 7 and plans to mark it by flashing a two-fingered peace sign and playing an evening gig at [New York's] Radio City Music Hall. He embarks this week on a three-week promotional tour for his just-released *Y Not* album, his 15th solo outing. *Y Not* continues a tradition begun on his last solo album, 2008's *Liverpool 8*, in which Starr includes an autobiographical song about his early life.

Rockin' Ringo: Drumming is still a passion with Ringo, especially if he's playing with his mates.

This time it's "The Other Side of Liverpool," which portrays his lower-working-class upbringing in "a cold and damp" city where the only way out was "drums, guitar and amp." "It was a tough, violent neighborhood," Starr says of The Dingle, then softens that a bit: "If you fell over in the street as a kid, everyone in that street was your mother and would come out and look after you. It's like fantasy now. But the thing I wrote this song for is that people believe I was born, joined The Beatles and then lived in a mansion."

That career-long frustration thankfully hasn't soured his relationship with his remaining mate, Paul McCartney, whom Starr invited to play on *Y Not*. "He's still one of the finest, most melodic bass players ever." Sir Paul played bass on "Peace Dream" and then unexpectedly offered a cute twist for the single "Walk With You," an ode to friendship on which McCartney echoes Starr's vocals one beat behind. "I had this little idea for a harmony on "Walk With You," says McCartney, "and I said, 'You probably don't want this, but let me show you this idea.' And he liked it, and so I ended up singing some harmonies. He's great to work with. He always was and always will be."

—Jerry Shriver

Voice-over: From 1984 to 1986, Ringo was the narrator of the TV show *Thomas the Tank Engine & Friends*. Here, he poses with Thomas.

Ringo's first marriage ended in 1975. He later married Barbara Bach, an actress. Children know Ringo as the voice of the narrator of their favorite animated show *Thomas the Tank Engine & Friends*.

All The Beatles were active in charities and other important causes. Before his death, John Lennon often helped groups devoted to peace. Yoko Ono continued that tradition, including donating money to the City of New York to create a memorial to John with a Strawberry Fields peace garden in Central Park.

Paul McCartney has been active in a number of causes, including the fight against breast cancer, a disease that claimed the life of his wife, Linda, in 1999. In 2002, Paul married former model Heather Mills, an anti-landmine activist from Great Britain. They had a daughter together in 2003 and divorced in 2008.

George Harrison's Concert for Bangladesh brought some of the world's best rock musicians together to raise money for Bangladesh, a small country ravaged by civil war and natural disasters.

Time Passing

The surviving band members continued to see one another and occasionally collaborated on projects. In the early 1990s, George, Paul, and Ringo began a huge collaboration—*The Beatles Anthology*. It was planned as a documentary that would also eventually involve a coffee-table book and rereleasing Beatles' music on CDs.

But another part of the *Anthology* involved "Free as a Bird," a song John had taped before his death. The surviving Beatles went into the studio to weave in additional music and lyrics. The resulting single has John on piano and singing, with Paul and George doing harmony, and Ringo keeping the beat.

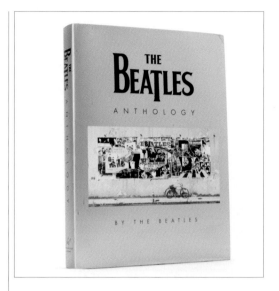

Coffee-table book: After the TV documentary aired in 1995, *The Beatles Anthology* book appeared in 2000. It included interviews that didn't make it into the documentary.

USA TODAY Snapshots®

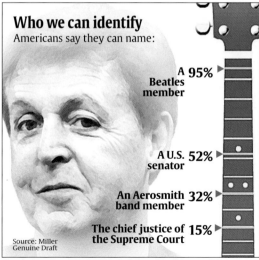

Who we can identify

Americans say they can name:

A **95%** Beatles member

A U.S. **52%** senator

An Aerosmith **32%** band member

The chief justice of **15%** the Supreme Court

Source: Miller Genuine Draft

Photo by Anne Ryan, USA TODAY By Beth Liu and Frank Pompa, USA TODAY, 2002

September 3, 1996

Anthology video spurs yet another Beatles blitz

From the Pages of
USA TODAY

"This video set is the cultural equivalent of the *Encyclopaedia Britannica*," Capitol Records executive Bruce Kirkland says of the eight-volume *Beatles Anthology*. "Every home needs one on the shelf." Applied to most entertainment phenomena, such a statement ranks as blatant hyperbole [overstatement]. In reference to the Fab Four, it's just telling it like it is.

The 10-hour *Beatles Anthology*, 5½ hours fatter than last fall's three-part ABC documentary, arrives in stores Thursday. Poised to spend $15 million on marketing, Capitol has high expectations. With good reason. Beatlemania remains an epidemic 30 years after the band's heyday.

An estimated 420 million people in 94 countries saw last year's documentary, including 60 million viewers in the USA. In December, *The Beatles Anthology 1* sold 855,797 in seven days, a record for a double album and history's highest-grossing first-week sales ($22 million). The second volume, out in March, sold 442,000 copies in one week and reignited sales of *Anthology 1*, the "Free as a Bird" single and previous albums. So far, the sets have sold a combined 16 million copies. The final installment is due Oct. 22.

Surveying the unstoppable popularity of the band, the *London Observer* wrote earlier this year, "The Beatles have achieved what every group since them has failed to do: become bigger than the Beatles."

Stuart Snyder, executive vice president of Turner Home Entertainment, dismisses concerns that fans will be sated by the TV version. "We're releasing the main course. People who saw the documentary haven't seen anything yet. On television, you had a presentation with commercial edits. From packaging to content, the video set is done by the Beatles, not ABC, not Turner, not Capitol. And it's an entirely seamless new production with more in-depth history, recording sessions, home movies and concert footage. Translation: expect a cross-generational buying frenzy.

—Edna Gundersen

Together again: Working on *Anthology* gave *(left to right)* Ringo, Paul, and George opportunities to visit and work in the studio again. Their friendship seemed to have survived the bad times.

The record—the first new Beatles' record in more than twenty-five years—did well on the music charts and even won a 1997 Grammy Award for Best Pop Performance by a Duo or Group.

The band members realized that a new generation of young people had come to love The Beatles. In fact, *Love* was the name of a Cirque du Soleil show based on music of The Beatles, remastered by none other than Sir George Martin and his son Giles. Giles also worked on the hugely anticipated *The Beatles: Rock Band*, a video game in which players can simulate performing as one of the band.

September 4, 2009

With 'Rock Band' game and remastered songs, The Beatles aim to enhance their legacy

<u>From the Pages of USA TODAY</u>

Beatlemania 2.0 looks and sounds a lot like the '60s prototype. Only crisper, clearer, shinier. The shrieking girls, the shaggy mop tops and their scores of indelible pop hits are digitally reborn in *The Beatles: Rock Band* video game, which hits store shelves Wednesday along with the band's newly remastered catalog, a long-awaited sonic upgrade of 14 titles.

"We're quite fussy," Paul McCartney tells USA TODAY, explaining why fans had to wait so long for the refurbished sounds of the iconic band that broke up nearly 40 years ago. "It's not as if we were going to crap out or sell out."

Ringo Starr serves up a cheeky pitch. "The game is great, the music's greater and, animated, I look gorgeous!" the drummer says of his video-game debut, The Beatles' first big marketing splash since 2006's Cirque du Soleil spectacle *Love*.

The masses remain mesmerized because "the music stands up," Starr says. "It's not the silly haircuts or the shoes or the suits. New generations of musicians and fans are still talking about that music."

Embedded in our cultural DNA, The Beatles have never lost their standing as the world's most influential and popular band. They've sold more records than any act in U.S. history, with 170 million shipped, according to the Recording Industry Association of America. They've sold 57.7 million albums since SoundScan began tracking U.S. sales in 1991.

The video game, a montage of animated performances that traces the group from its beginnings in Liverpool to its bittersweet final performance on a London rooftop in 1969, "appealed to me because it's a different way of presenting The Beatles' music, just as *Love* is," says McCartney.

"I realize how important this is to a generation," he says. "And behind them is the next generation. When I told people we were doing *Rock Band*, their eyes would light up. I could feed off their excitement. Our role was to get the spirit as near to the reality as we could. The music was still in the hands of Giles (Martin, son of storied Beatles producer George Martin and the producer who remixed 45 songs for the video game) and engineers who'd always been with The Beatles. There was a lot of continuity. It was as carefully crafted as our records were."

Though steered toward simultaneous release, the game and the remasters evolved on radically different paths. In Beatle time, *Rock Band* materialized overnight. Fans started pining for a digital overhaul of the Beatles catalog soon after its transfer to CD 22 years ago. Four years ago, engineers at EMI's Abbey Road Studios began importing the music from analog tapes to digital files using state-of-the-art technology and vintage gear. Many fans

Rock band: Ringo *(left)* and Paul *(right)* took center stage when *The Beatles: Rock Band* video game was introduced in 2009.

complained that the sonic scrub was long overdue, but Harrison suggests the timing was ideal. "A lot of early remastered music sounded brittle," she says. "These are very warm and clear. They don't sound messed with. It's like they cleaned them but left the ambience."

The new versions "are more like what we heard coming out of the speakers as we made the records," McCartney says. "It's like being in the studio again. It's exciting, particularly considering the passing of John and George. I can hear them so clearly."

Smacked by the first wave of Beatlemania 46 years ago, McCartney expected a short ride. "Oh, yeah, we thought a couple years, that would be it," he says. "We never thought it would last at all. You've got to ask, 'Why did it last?' I think the music is very well-structured, like a good house. It's going to stand for a long time. It's nice that I can sit back now and be proud of what we did. And feel very privileged to be one of four guys who did it."

—Edna Gundersen

George Harrison was the second Beatle to die. In 1999 he survived an attack on his life when a mentally ill man broke into Friar Park and stabbed him. His wife Olivia saved his life by struggling with the intruder and scaring him away. For many years, George had struggled with health problems caused by smoking cigarettes, and the attack weakened his lungs further. He died of cancer on November 29, 2001, with Olivia and his son, Dhani, by his side.

For all their individual success, none of The Beatles' solo albums or songs have the same impact as those they made as a group. The reasons are many. The Beatles came of age at a very special time. Changes in technology and society, along with the arrival of the baby boom generation, helped set the stage for them. As The Beatles, they created music that was about their time but would last beyond their time.

Combined genius: Four lads—with different skills and personalities but bound by a common background—gave the world music that has stood the test of time.

October 2, 2003

'Concert for George' is treasured tribute to the former Beatle

From the Pages of USA TODAY

When George Harrison died, he left musical gems, treasured friends and a wealth of devoted fans. Eric Clapton, serving as musical director, leads a stellar cast of musicians through Harrison's spiritually vibrant songbook. Billy Preston sings "My Sweet Lord." Paul McCartney accompanies himself on ukulele for "Something." Ringo Starr revives "Photograph," which he co-wrote with Harrison. Jeff Lynne does "Inner Light" and "Give Me Love."

George's friends: Olivia *(left)* and Dhani *(right)* Harrison organized the Concert for George. It brought together musicians who were lifelong friends of the former Beatle.

"Everyone you see on the stage was an actual close friend," says Tom Petty, who joined The Heartbreakers on "Taxman" and on the Traveling Wilburys tune "Handle With Care." Concert for George "certainly serves his spirit," Petty says.

After Harrison died of cancer at 58, his widow, Olivia, and Clapton teamed to produce a fitting toast to the former Beatle's life and music. The players practiced songs for three weeks before taking the incense-scented stage in front of cameras and a packed house. A huge portrait of Harrison loomed overhead.

"Nobody wanted to mess up," says Lynne, co-producer of Harrison's swan-song album, *Brainwashed*. "Everyone was familiar with his songs, but most of us hadn't played them before. It was a learning experience."

Dhani Harrison plays guitar through much of the concert and says his father "would have had a good old time seeing how mad we were over him."

—Robert Bianco

The group combined the genius and talents of the individual members, as well as the skills of others like George Martin. George Harrison's sweet guitar and Ringo Starr's steady beat were every bit as important as the lead singers' harmonies. The tension between John's and Paul's different approaches was a necessary part of their success as songwriters. Ringo gave the others important advice on what worked or didn't work musically. The collaboration of different attitudes and experiences produced unique music. In this case, the old cliché "the sum is greater than the parts" was true.

It was not always a smooth relationship, but even with the bad feelings that surrounded the band's breakup, some part of the complicated friendship managed to survive. In his book, *The Beatles Album*, Geoffrey Giuliano tells a story about John Lennon. A young woman saw him one day in New York City in

USA TODAY Snapshots®

Beatlemania at the bookstore

Books published about the Fab Four:

44¹

2006 · 23
2005 · 30
2004 · 30
2003

Source:
Compiled by
Andrew Grabois,
Books in Print

1 — Preliminary; includes books published and announced through November

By Jacqueline Blais and Bob Laird, USA TODAY, 2006

the 1970s. He was wearing a vintage "I Love Paul" button from the days of Beatlemania. At the time, many newspaper stories said that John Lennon and Paul McCartney hated each other. So the woman asked John why he was wearing the button. "Because I love Paul," he told her.

Love fades but somehow survives. And so does The Beatles' music.

SOURCE NOTES

12 Hunter Davies, *The Beatles* (New York: W. W. Norton & Co., 1996), 21.

13 Ibid., 20.

14 Barry Miles, *Paul McCartney—Many Years from Now* (New York: Henry Holt and Company, 1997), 52.

15 Telegraph Media Group, "Sir Paul McCartney Denies He Did Not Get on with John Lennon." August 25, 2009, http://www.telegraph. co.uk/culture/music/music-news/6083346/Sir-Paul-McCartney-denies-he-did-not-get-on-with-John-Lennon.html (September 2, 2010).

15 Davies, *The Beatles*, 70.

16 David Pritchard and Alan Lysaght, *The Beatles: An Oral History* (New York: Hyperion, 1998), 41.

17 Bob Cepican and Waleed Ali, *Yesterday Came Suddenly* (New York: Arbor House, 1985), 71–72.

20 Miles, *Paul McCartney*, 74.

20 David Sheff, *The Playboy Interviews with John Lennon and Yoko Ono* (New York: Playboy Press, 1981), 142.

23 Brian Epstein, *A Cellarful of Noise* (New York: Pocket Books, 1998), 105.

25 Ray Coleman, *The Man Who Made The Beatles—an Intimate Biography of Brian Epstein* (New York: McGraw-Hill, 1989), 97–98.

25 Davies, *The Beatles*, 135.

29–30 Ray Coleman, *Lennon—the Definitive Biography* (New York: HarperPerennial, 1992), 264.

29 Davies, *The Beatles*, 151.

30 Ibid., 163.

30 Ibid.

30 Ibid., 164.

31 David Sheff, *The Playboy Interviews,* 116.

31 Ross Benson, *"Paul McCartney—Beyond the Myth."* (London: Victor Gollancz, 1992), 178.

31 George Martin, *"With a Little Help from My Friends"* (New York: Little Brown and Company, 1994), 98.

33 Pritchard and Lysaght, *The Beatles: An Oral History*, 118.

33–34 Philip Norman, *Shout! The Beatles in Their Generation* (New York: Simon and Schuster, 1981), 177.

36 *The Complete Beatles*, VHS, directed by P. Montgomery and Stephanie Bennett (Teleculture, 1982).

36 Gareth L. Pawlowski, *How They Became The Beatles* (New York: E. P. Dutton, 1989), 130.

37 Davies, *The Beatles*, 184.

40 Cepican and Ali, *Yesterday Came Suddenly*, 148.

41 Davies, *The Beatles*, 196.

52–53 Geoffrey Giuliano and Brenda Giuliano, *The Lost Beatles Interviews* (New York: Dutton, 1994), 69.

53 Coleman, *Lennon*, 408.

53 Ibid., 410–411.

56 Miles, *Paul McCartney,* 202

58 Pritchard and Lysaght, *The Beatles, an Oral History*, 233–234.

59 Norman, *Shout! The Beatles*, 288.

62 Martin, *With a Little Help from My Friends*, 104.

66 Pritchard and Lysaght, *The Beatles: An Oral History*, 109.

66 Coleman, *The Man Who Made The Beatles*, 382.

67 Miles, *Paul McCartney*, 368.

67 Norman, *Shout! The Beatles*, 317.

69 David Sheff, quoted in Richard Buskin, *John Lennon, His Life and Legend* (Lincolnwood, IL: Publications International, 1991), 152.

70 Miles, *Paul McCartney*, 427.

73 Coleman, *Lennon*, 488.

74 Norman, *Shout! The Beatles,* 320.

75 Ibid., 360.

77 Mark Lewisohn, *The Complete Beatles Chronicle* (London: Pyramid Books, 1992), 310.

77 Ibid.

77 Ibid., 311.

81 Martin, *With a Little Help from My Friends*, 139.

82 Miles, *Paul McCartney*, 552.

83 Norman, *Shout! The Beatles,* 385.

85 Dorothy Bacon, "The Case of the 'Missing' Beatle: Paul Is Still with Us," *Life*, November 7, 1969, 105.

88 Coleman, *Lennon*, 679.

102 Geoffrey Giuliano, *The Beatles Album* (New York: Viking Studio Books, 1991), 218.

SELECTED BIBLIOGRAPHY

Bacon, David, and Norman Maslov. *The Beatles' England*. San Francisco: Nine Hundred Ten Press, 1982.

Benson, Ross. *Paul McCartney—Beyond the Myth*. London: Victor Gollancz, 1992.

Brown, Peter, and Steven Gaines. *The Love You Make*. New York: McGraw-Hill, 1983.

Cepican, Bob, and Waleed Ali. *Yesterday Came Suddenly*. New York: Arbor House, 1985.

Clayson, Alan. *Ringo Starr: Straight Man or Joker?* New York: Paragon House, 1992.

Coleman, Ray. *Lennon—the Definitive Biography*. New York: HarperPerennial, 1992.

Davies, Hunter. *The Beatles*. New York: W. W. Norton & Company, 1996.

Epstein, Brian. *A Cellarful of Noise*. New York: Pocket Books, 1998.

Giuliano, Geoffrey. *The Beatles Album*. New York: Viking Studio Book, 1991.

Giuliano, Geoffrey, and Brenda Giuliano. *The Lost Beatles Interviews*. New York: Dutton, 1994.

Harrison, George. *I, Me, Mine*. New York: Simon and Schuster, 1980.

Lewisohn, Mark. *The Complete Beatles Chronicle*. London: Pyramid Books, 1992.

Miles, Barry. *Paul McCartney—Many Years from Now*. New York: Henry Holt and Company, 1997.

Neises, Charles P., ed. *The Beatles Reader*. Ann Arbor, MI: Pierian Press, 1984.

Norman, Philip. *Shout! The Beatles in Their Generation*. New York: Simon and Schuster, 1981.

Pawlowski, Gareth L. *How They Became The Beatles*. New York: E. P. Dutton, 1989.

Pritchard, David, and Alan Lysaght. *The Beatles: An Oral History*. New York: Hyperion, 1998.

AN INTRODUCTORY DISCOGRAPHY

BRITISH RELEASES

Please Please Me, Parlophone Records, 1963.

With The Beatles, Parlophone Records, 1963.

A Hard Day's Night, Parlophone Records, 1964.

Beatles for Sale, Parlophone Records, 1964.

Help!, Parlophone Records, 1965.

Rubber Soul, Parlophone Records, 1965.

Revolver, Parlophone Records, 1966.

A Collection of Beatles Oldies, Parlophone Records, 1966.

Sgt. Pepper's Lonely Hearts Club Band, Parlophone Records, 1967.

The Beatles, Apple Records, 1968.

Yellow Submarine, Apple Records, 1969.

Abbey Road, Apple Records, 1969.

Let It Be, Apple Records, 1970.

The Beatles 1962–1966, Apple Records, 1973.

The Beatles 1967–1970, Apple Records, 1973.

The Beatles Live! At the Star-Club in Hamburg, Germany; 1962, Lingasong, 1977.

The Beatles at the Hollywood Bowl, Parlophone Records, 1977.

Past Masters, Volumes One and Two, Apple Corps/EMI, 1988.

The Beatles Anthology, Volumes 1, 2, and 3, Apple Corps/EMI, 1995, 1996.

U.S. RELEASES

Introducing The Beatles, Vee Jay Records, 1963.

Meet the Beatles!, Capitol Records, 1964.

The Beatles' Second Album, Capitol Records, 1964.

A Hard Day's Night, United Artists Records, 1964.

Something New, Capitol Records, 1964.

The Beatles' Story, Capitol Records, 1964 (a documentary sound track with interviews) Beatles '65, Capitol Records, 1964.

The Early Beatles, Capitol Records, 1965 (contains many songs from the British *Please Please Me* album).

Beatles VI, Capitol Records, 1965.

Help!, Capitol Records, 1965.

Rubber Soul, Capitol Records, 1965.

Yesterday and Today, Capitol Records, 1966.

Revolver, Capitol Records, 1966.

Sgt. Pepper's Lonely Hearts Club Band, Capitol Records, 1967.

Magical Mystery Tour, Capitol Records, 1967.

The Beatles, Apple Records, 1968.

Yellow Submarine, Apple Records, 1969.

Abbey Road, Apple Records, 1969.

Let It Be, Apple Records, 1970.

The Beatles 1962–1966, Apple Records, 1973.

The Beatles 1967–1970, Apple Records, 1973.

The Beatles Live! At the Star Club in Hamburg, Germany: 1962, Lingasong, 1977.

The Beatles at the Hollywood Bowl, Parlophone Records, 1977.

Past Masters Volumes One and Two, Apple Corps/EMI, 1988.

The Beatles Anthology, Volumes 1, 2, and 3, Apple Corps/EMI, 1995, 1996.

The Beatles 1, EMI/Capitol, 2000.

Let It Be . . . Naked, Capitol, 2003.

Love, Capitol, 2006.

Past Masters, Capitol, 2009.

The Beatles: Rock Band, a music video game; Wii, 2009.

FILMOGRAPHY

FILMS FEATURING THE BEATLES
A Hard Day's Night, directed by Richard Lester, United Artists, 1964.

Help!, directed by Richard Lester, United Artists, 1965.

Magical Mystery Tour, directed by Dennis O'Dell, Apple Films, 1968.

Yellow Submarine, directed by George Dunning, MGA/UA, 1968.

DOCUMENTARIES ON THE BEATLES
The Compleat Beatles, directed by P. Montgomery and Stephanie Bennett, Teleculture, 1982.

Get Back, directed by Jordan Croneweth and Robert Paynter, Vestron Video, 1991.

The Beatles Anthology, directed by Geoff Wohfor, Capitol Video, 1996.

FURTHER READING AND WEBSITES

Books
Anderson, Jennifer Joline. *John Lennon: Legendary Musician and Beatle.* Edina, MN: ABDO Publishing Company, 2009.

Campbell, Kumari. *United Kingdom in Pictures*. Minneapolis, Twenty-First Century Books, 2004.

Delaney, Mark. *Pepperland*. Atlanta: Peachtree Publishers, 2004.

Duggleby, John. *Revolution: The Story of John Lennon*. Greensboro, NC: Morgan Reynolds Publishing, 2007.

Gallagher, Jim. *The Beatles*. Broomall, PA: Mason Street Publishers, 2007.

Glassman, Bruce S. *John Lennon and Paul McCartney: Their Magic and Their Music*. Farmington Hills, MI: Cengage Gale, 1995.

Lalani, Zane. *Teenagers Guide to the Beatles*. Tampa: AverStream Press, 2005.

Lindop, Edmund, and Margaret J. Goldstein. *America in the 1960s*. Minneapolis: Twenty-First Century Books, 2010.

Spitz, Bob. *Yeah! Yeah! Yeah!: The Beatles, Beatlemania, and the Music That Changed the World*. New York: Little, Brown, 2007.

Websites

The Beatles' England

http://www.music.indiana.edu/som/courses/rock/england.html
This site offers photos and descriptions of different sites that were important to The Beatles, including birthplaces, homes, clubs where they performed, recording studios, and other places of interest.

The Beatles Ultimate Experience

http://www.beatlesinterviews.org/
This database offers hundreds of interviews with The Beatles. It also includes many photos.

George Harrison

http://www.georgeharrison.com/
As the official site of the former Beatle, this site has videos, a discography, and information about Harrison's charities.

John Lennon

http://www.johnlennon.com/html/biography.aspx
Created by Yoko Ono, this official John Lennon site includes a biography, videos, photos, and much more.

Paul McCartney

http://www.paulmccartney.com/
The official site of the former Beatle features news, videos, and information about McCartney's tours.

Ringo Starr

http://www.ringostarr.com/
This official site of the former drummer for The Beatles includes a biography, photographs, videos, and much more.

PHOTO ACKNOWLEDGMENTS

The images in this book are used with the permission of: © Evening Standard/Hulton Archive/Getty Images, pp. 1, 84; © Terence Spencer/Camera Press Digital/Retna Ltd., p. 2; © Keystone/Hulton Archive/Getty Images, pp. 4, 14, 33, 45; AP Photo/Str, p. 5; AP Photo/stf, p. 6; © John Dominis/Time & Life Pictures/Getty Images, p. 7; © Nat Farbman/Time & Life Pictures/Getty Images, p. 8; © Pictorial Press/Hulton Archive/ Getty Images, p. 9 (left); © Photofest, pp. 9 (right), 23, 28; © Globe Photos, Inc., p. 10; © Michael Ochs Archives/Getty Images, pp. 13, 18 (top), 29, 40, 57 (left), 60, 63, 75, 82, 90 (top), 93 (top), 96, 98, 101 (top); © Astrid Kirchherr - K&K/Redferns/ Getty Images, p. 17; © Jurgen Vollmer/Redferns/Getty Images, p. 18 (bottom); © Mark and Colleen Hayward/Hulton Archive/Getty Images, p. 19; © Val Wilmer/ Redferns/Getty Images, p. 21; © Hulton Archive/Archive Photos/Getty Images, p. 22; © Bettmann/CORBIS, pp. 27, 52; AP Photo, pp. 32, 39, 46, 51; © USA TODAY, pp. 34, 91; © Michael Webb/Hulton Archive/Getty Images, p. 35; © George Freston/ Fox Photos/Hulton Archive/Getty Images, p. 37; © Fox Photos/Hulton Archive/Getty Images, p. 43; Everett Collection, pp. 44, 68, 74, 79, 86; © Hulton Archive/Getty Images, p. 47; © Jan Olofsson/Redferns/Getty Images, p. 54; © Terry Disney/Express/ Hulton Archive/Getty Images, p. 57 (right); © RDImages/Epics/Hulton Archive/Getty Images, p. 58; Mirrorpix/Courtesy Everett Collection, p. 61; © Keystone Features/ Hulton Archive/Getty Images, p. 62; © Cummings Archives/Redferns/Getty Images, p. 65; AP Photo/Don Ryan, p. 66; © Central Press/Hulton Archive/Getty Images, p. 67; © John Pratt/Keystone/Hulton Archive/Getty Images, p. 70; © Express/Archive Photos/Hulton Archive/Getty Images, p. 76; © Jan Persson/Redferns/Getty Images, p. 80; © Oli Scarff/Getty Images, p. 81; Cleveland Public Library/Everett Collection, p. 83; © Stan Honda/AFP/Getty Images, p. 88; © Stringer/Getty Images, p. 89; AP Photo/Denis O'Regan/Pool, p. 90 (bottom); © Dave Benett/Hulton Archive/Getty Images, pp. 92, 101 (bottom); © Brad Barket/Getty Images, p. 93 (bottom); ITV/ Rex USA/Everett Collection, p. 94; © H. Darr Beiser/USA TODAY, p. 95 (top); © Tom Hanley/Redferns/Getty Images, p. 97; © Robert Hanashiro/USA TODAY, p. 99; Press Association via AP Photo, p. 100.

Front cover: © Terence Spencer/Camera Press/Retna Ltd.
Back cover: Everett Collection.

ABOUT THE AUTHOR

Jeremy Roberts is the pen name of Jim DeFelice. He often uses this name when he writes for young readers, which he tries to do as much as he can. Besides this book, his nonfiction books include works on skydiving and rock climbing. He has written several installments in the Eerie, Indiana series and quite a few horror tales. His adult books include a historical trilogy and techno-thrillers. He lives with his wife and son in upstate New York.